RESET:

MAKE THE MOST OF YOUR STRESS

Your 24-7 Plan for Well-Being

Dr. Kristen Lee Costa

iUniverse®

RESET: MAKE THE MOST OF YOUR STRESS
YOUR 24-7 PLAN FOR WELL-BEING

Author Credits: Kristen Lee Costa
Cover design and inside graphics by Kenneth Fontaine
Author photo by Charles E. Wingate, III

iUniverse books may be ordered through booksellers or by contacting:

iUniverse
1663 Liberty Drive
Bloomington, IN 47403
www.iuniverse.com
1-800-Authors (1-800-288-4677)

The information and guidance presented in this book are not meant to be a substitute for the advice of your physician and or other trained mental health care professionals. You are advised to consult with licensed health care professionals regarding all matters that may require mental health, medical attention or diagnosis and to check with a physician or licensed practitioner before administering or undertaking any course of treatment.

Examples provided throughout the book are composites, comprised by combining similar anecdotes provided by individuals. Incidents and composites are presented so as to disguise actual identity and protect confidentiality.

ISBN: 978-1-4917-4755-1 (sc)
ISBN: 978-1-4917-4757-5 (hc)
ISBN: 978-1-4917-4756-8 (e)

Library of Congress Control Number: 2014917294

Printed in the United States of America.

iUniverse rev. date: 10/31/2014

To Grandma J—the definition of resilience.

To the cast of characters in my life: thank you for the simultaneous bursts of confidence and humility you instill in me.

Contents

Part 3
Maintaining Your Sense of Well-Being: Your RESET Plan of Action

The Man Who Ate a Plane

When the well's dry, we know the worth of water.
—Ben Franklin

"No bananas for me!" cried the Frenchman, not to be distracted from his main course. "Bring on the bolts!"

It was 1978 when Michel Lotito's appetite for indigestible objects got the best of him. It wasn't enough that he had already purposely devoured bicycles, shopping carts, and razor blades. For two years, Monsieur Mangetout—or "Mr. Eats All"—devoted himself to eating a Cessna 150 aircraft. Two pounds daily brought him to his goal, adding to his nine-ton lifetime tally of metal (and perhaps mental) mayhem.

What made this possible? Mr. Eats All apparently had unique attributes contributing toward his record-breaking binges. His super-Charmin-cushioned stomach and eccentricities helped him defy convention.

But there's more to it.

Mr. Eats All understood the importance of *slow digestion*. Bit by bit, he was somehow able to tolerate the distress he willfully invited. Even with his stomach of steel, slugging down the pieces would have been dicey if he had gone over his two-pound limit. He could process the foreign objects only in manageable chunks. He knew when to say "when."

This is not something I recommend doing at home, but there are lessons within this story of culinary chaos. Despite Mr. Eats All's ingestion of toxic materials, his tank remained resilient, and he found his *maximum threshold* for how much he could process. Adult life leaves us having to digest overwhelming amounts of information. Stress doesn't come in neatly packaged rations; we're forced to process change, loss, and harsh realities in heaping portions. Like our stomachs, our brains have limits to what they can effectively tolerate. Massive stress can leave our minds churning and on a hunt to find some sort of solace.

So what's the remedy? Most of us have to digest things we'd rather not. Things that puncture us and keep us awake at night. Things we prefer not to mention to others. Things that seem to be beyond what we can handle. In the middle of all of this, it's easy to be so consumed by our worries that we forget something essential to our emotional survival: we need *time* and *tools* to better take care of ourselves—*before, during,* and *after* the storms hit.

As we'll see, *being able to maintain well-being in the face of stress requires deliberate action.* It's not about rapid digestion, a specific formula, or having "perfect" reactions to what comes your way. It's not about how your friends or family cope, or how they say that *you* should—but what makes sense to you personally. RESET is a tool I've developed over many years as a therapist and teacher to help you understand your stress threshold and find ways to cope even when life seems completely out of control. It helps you build your own unique definition of "self-care" and put it into action.

When you're feeling beyond your limits, RESET's five components will help you get your bearings and recalibrate:

Realize.
Energize.
Soothe.
End unproductive thinking.
Talk it out.

Whether you know it or not, you're already responding to stress—either constructively or destructively. By creating a plan that is unique to your own set of circumstances, you'll be better equipped to respond to the challenges before you.

How can you possibly begin to digest what life brings?

It's time to find out.

ACKNOWLEDGMENTS

Writing a book requires a measure of resilience that wouldn't be possible without the enduring support of wonderful colleagues, friends, and family.

I first thank those who bravely came to me for therapy, whose stories and experiences compelled me to create the first version of RESET. You have been with me through this entire writing process, and I hold you dear in my heart.

I also thank my students, whose eagerness and curiosity propel me forward.

I've stood on the shoulders of giants who have inspired me and influenced my work. Thank you to Brené Brown, Peggy Ramundo, Kate Kelly, Edward Hallowell, Deirdre V. Lovecky, John Ratey, Thom Hartmann, Lois Weiner, Ross Greene, Harriet Lerner, Carol Dweck, Jonathan Mooney, Sam Goldstein, and Robert Brooks.

Thank you to my local librarians who (mostly) spare me the evil eyebrow on my late fines and who don't raise too many questions about my gluttony for the human help genre. Or maybe you're nice because you're worried that I'm a bit off-kilter.

Several friends and colleagues generously offered their time and expertise throughout various stages of this endeavor. A special shout-out to Jane Lohmann, Kathleen Mackenzie, Cameron Marzelli, Jackie Shannon, Dolores Hirschmann, Douglas Flor, Evangeline Harris-Stefanakis, and Carol Radford for your pizazz and for believing in our shared work with such conviction.

To Leslie Cohen, editor extraordinaire, I'm truly grateful that our paths have crossed. In addition to your fine eye for detail, your encouragement and affirmations have meant a great deal.

My career path has been shaped profoundly by many wonderful mentors, practitioners, and scholars whom I've had the good fortune of deliberating with. Thanks to Scott Thompson, Eva Havas, Lydia Breckon Smith, Odete Amarelo, Elaine Oliveira, Nancy Castino, Deborah Herrmann, Lydia Trow, Edgardo Angeles, Catalina Angeles, Vangie Dizon, Nancy Harper, Denise Porché, Lisa St. Laurent, Karen O'Connor, Katherine Gaudet, and all of my NU colleagues for what you bring out in me.

Nate Hall and Mark Gelinas, you exemplify love. Your faith, wisdom, and humility are needed gifts in my life.

To my dear friends, you bring so much light. Heidi Maxwell, Karen McNary, Shelly Roy, Lisa Densman, Dianne Mazzocca, Jacqueline Campos, Seema and Tom Vallone, and Vanda and Alan Blinn—I am blessed to share the journey with you.

To Ken Fontaine—your depth is astounding. Thank you for generously sharing your inspiration with me.

I breathe a huge sigh of relief as I think about the ways in which Lyla Fanger, Jean Peelor, Kathy Benevides, Becky Costa, Ken Branco, and the Sailor Shiatsu therapist on the mountain (oh, the elation!) have helped me manage my own self-care process.

For my entire family, who entertain my ideas and give me the enthusiasm to press forward, I thank you deeply. To my whole crew of siblings, in-laws, nephews, nieces—you guys give me lots of good material! To Eduardo and Ana, thanks for your support and for raising such a terrific son. Thanks for the pictures, Amber. Thanks especially to Harry, Maura, Lenny, and Amanda for your genuine interest and funny ways. To my parents, Michael and Gail Lee, who tell anyone who can't escape fast enough about my work, thanks for believing in me. To Scott, Tori, and Ryan, the joy you bring is immeasurable. You've taught me the *most* about resetting. Scott, I adore you in every sense. Thanks for being a (mostly) willing accomplice on endless adventures and for appreciating my elf ways.

Finally, thank you, God, for the struggles and successes you've allowed me.

Uneasy ...

An ounce of prevention is worth a pound of cure.
—Ben Franklin

ESSENTIAL QUESTION: What is your current
stress level, and how are you managing it?

Where's my reset button?

In August 2005, Staples launched its now-famous "That Was Easy" slogan as a clever attempt to remedy stress. With a tidal wave of sales, the button made its way into millions of homes and offices, providing comic relief and spurring wishful thinking.

If only life were that simple. I've counseled thousands who are looking for some version of a reset button. Life is filled with constant change, stress, and demands. Most people enter therapy, or attempt self-help, at a crumbling point. They want a neat, mobile, cookie-cutter, five-step approach for well-being. Generally, people think we therapists have some sort of Jedi power or magical wand. No pressure.

Like other mental health professionals, I have had a lot of experience helping people cope with what's bothering them. They trust my guidance. But they don't want long-winded answers and complicated advice. They need to be heard and supported to find ways to build on their strengths and cope with what's at hand—whether *everyday stressors* or *severe crises*. We all need self-care strategies to help mitigate the harmful toll that stress can take. Many of us end up neglecting self-care at the very moment we need to keep track of it the most.

Term	Definition	CONSIDER THIS
Self-care	Being aware of a wide range of personal needs and deliberately taking action to support our own well-being.	Neglecting this can lead to difficulty. Being physically, mentally, emotionally, and spiritually strong relies on our commitment to taking care of ourselves in all of these ways.

A new framework for self-care: RESET

While explaining the definition of self-care in a therapy session to a woman who needed concrete, realistic goals, I sketched out the word "RESET" and a rough framework to help her put self-care into action. This was how RESET was born.

After she left, I realized how easy to remember it was, and I began making it my quest to develop a model that was anchored in clinical knowledge *and* useful in the face of life's various zingers. With that goal in mind, I developed the RESET model to provide a framework that helps keep us on track with our efforts to stay emotionally healthy.

RESET is based on the premise that our brains and bodies benefit from engaging in productive thinking, exercise, enjoyable activities, and positive connections. It has universal application and is helpful for stressors of varying degrees. RESET provides a framework for wellness for a range of situations and, when practiced regularly, can help improve adaption in a host of circumstances. RESET is driven by proven, research-based models, including

- the latest neuroscience research on exercise and movement;
- cognitive behavioral therapy (CBT);
- dialectical behavioral therapy (DBT); and
- appreciative inquiry (AI) and strengths-based perspective.

As we all know, there's no shortage of five-step programs, gimmicks, self-help, and pop psychology to go around. RESET is designed to transcend the latest fad or technique. I purposely try to avoid psychobabble, trite slogans, or therapeutic jargon that either makes sense only to a few elite professionals or holds few new insights. There are far too many books and plans that are either too *complicated* or too *simple* to really make an impact. I wanted something driven by useful treatment models to remember and follow.

Since the inception of RESET, I not only have tried to practice the principles regularly but also have shared the concepts with thousands who find themselves constantly trying to respond to life's curveballs. So often, clusters of problems arrive at our doorstep—leaving us frazzled, depleted, and ready to snap. Sometimes it's a matter of the sheer pace of life today, and other times, it's devastating events like cancer, depression, divorce, death, financial collapse, oppression, and other intense versions of suffering.

Life is just plain hard, isn't it?

Whether you are dealing with everyday stress or major whoppers, learning self-care principles is vital for your health and happiness. I share these RESET concepts, which are practical, proven, and memorable, in the spirit of wanting to help you build the skills to manage your stress and improve your well-being. It won't be easy, but it is well worth the investment.

This book is divided into three simple parts, all emphasizing smart, research-driven approaches to well-being and keeping anxiety and emotional overload at bay.

First, in part 1, we'll talk about what leads to feeling stuck, looking at real-life examples to help make adjustments. Part 2 explains the RESET principles and ways to apply them to your own thinking and way of being. Finally, in part 3, we'll examine ways to measure what you're doing and implement your self-care plan. For those of you who don't prefer to read a book cover to cover, each chapter offers essential questions to ask yourself, bottom-line reminders, key definitions to consider, examples to dissect and reflect on, and end-of-chapter "In a Nutshell" summaries. Last, at the end of the book, you'll find a review of the key concepts I've written about, as well as many handy resources and recommendations to further support your growth and well-being.

Let's RESET!

PART 1

What Gets You Stuck?

ॐ The Many Sides of Stress ॐ

ॐ Saving the Swimmer ॐ

ॐ Therapy 101 ॐ

ॐ Sprinters, Skippers, Tumblers ॐ

ॐ There's No Golden Ticket ॐ

ॐ Calm Trees ॐ

1

THE MANY SIDES OF STRESS

Chasing meaning is better for your health
than trying to avoid discomfort.
—Kelly McGonical, PhD

ESSENTIAL QUESTION: In what ways can
anxiety help or hurt me?

There are scores of self-help messages telling us to run away from
stress and promising to eliminate it in three simple steps. This
is tempting, indeed, although recent scholars have poked holes in
this line of thinking. It turns out that efforts to avoid discomfort
altogether can bring on an entirely new set of struggles. When we're
out living life, taking risks and working toward our goals, we are likely
to find ourselves engulfed in some version of stress. This can cause us
to second-guess ourselves and start doing mental gymnastics over
how and why we've gotten ourselves into our latest predicament.
We may begin calculating our stress level and become increasingly
worried and overwhelmed as we inventory all the things that are
pressing upon us.

But research is proving that stress is a sign of healthy living,
engagement, productivity, and desire to improve ourselves and our

circumstances. Have you ever stopped to think that stress can be an amazing teacher and propel us into needed action? The natural anxiety that arises during life's difficult moments can actually bring on enough stress for us to focus and develop a game plan. Yet, without careful attention, stress can be all-consuming. Left untended, stress can lead to suboptimal mental health.

Clearly, stress is indeed paradoxical. It serves us well to think about the different sides of it—and what we can do to make the most of the anxiety that comes along with it.

The pros and cons of anxiety

Anxiety is not reserved for people who have full-fledged anxiety disorders but is often a very natural response to living. Think about what makes *you* anxious. If you worry about your job, it reflects *conscientiousness*. If you worry that you'll be sick, you value your *health*. If you worry about your family, it's because you *love* them. These worries demonstrate that you are actively engaging in life, wanting the best in your personal and professional lives, which takes a fair amount of courage. We can think of our concerns as "motivational anxieties" since they keep us on our toes, energized, and eager to find ways to improve and reach our goals.

On the other hand, when anxiety becomes too intense, it can wreak havoc. Anxiety can become so disruptive that it thrusts us into a cycle of self-defeating thinking and behavior. I've seen a lot of people needlessly neglect their own lives until the point of crisis. Hit with major challenges, we are likely to tumble off track and stop investing in self-care. It's often hard to admit that we are struggling, so we become reluctant to bring our struggles to anyone's attention. In doing this, we lose the opportunity to problem solve and get needed support. In other words, we compound our anxiety.

So anxiety is a two-edged sword: a powerful weapon—yet potentially dangerous if not handled well.

The two sides of anxiety

Motivational	Disruptive
Keeps you on your toes, motivated	Leaves you with a never-ending sense of urgency and feelings of failure and concern over performance and accomplishment
Can make you highly tuned in and sensitive with a strong sense of self-awareness, empathy	Disrupts your ability to see the big picture; leads to personalizing and frequent hurt feelings/anger
Alerts you to "danger" and helps you get out of troublesome situations	Interrupts comfort level in social interactions; can lead to isolation
Allows for in-depth analysis of people and problems	Rents all the space in your head, leading to distress and taking away from more productive thoughts and activities; "analysis paralysis" leaves you stuck and unable to see what alternative conclusions/ solutions are possible
Leads to careful decision making and high conscientiousness	Increases impulsivity and leads to rash decisions with negative outcomes like strained relationships or finances

As we see, anxiety—one result of stress—isn't always bad. There are similar physical parallels. For example, when our bodies get a fever, we should take appropriate measures, of course, but it's also important to realize that the fever is actually a sign that the body is fighting off an infection. Nature provides many mechanisms in our brains and bodies designed to restore us. When it comes to anxiety, sometimes we get stressed about being stressed without stopping and realizing the two sides of the coin. Without any stress, we would be so lackadaisical that we would get nothing done, and we wouldn't appreciate when things were going well. As they say, life might be boring!

We can often look back at difficulties and realize their purpose and value. In the moment, it's hard to embrace the positive side of problems, but time gives us a new perspective. In addition to seeing the truth of this for many that I've worked with, my own experiences reinforce this lesson. As I look back, I can see that some of my most significant bouts of stress were disruptive while they were occurring, but they led me to be more compassionate and less judgmental—which obviously comes in handy as a therapist! My difficult life experiences have contributed to my resilience and ability to keep my perspective in the face of both challenges (hanging in when it's tough) and triumphs (appreciating when things are smooth).

Learning from my own story

As is true for all the people I have worked with, there are two narratives or "sides of the story" regarding my anxiety, as well. One is that it can work in my favor, keeping me motivated and on task. I know what it's like to get into slumps and feel stuck, so I avoid that at all costs; but sometimes the price of going full-out can be high. I don't want to miss out on anything; whether it be reaching a goal or participating in an activity, I am full throttle. People comment, "You never stop," "I don't know how you do it," and "Where are the margins in your life?" I smile and say something along the lines of "My schedule keeps me out of trouble!" I know full well that I absolutely love the adrenaline and have a constant desire for more experiences, successes, and connections. I also realize that fear of losing traction drives my behavior and that I might lose momentum if my adrenaline level were to subside.

As with most high-achieving types, there is a flip side to being such a hypermotivated person, or what Dr. Harriet Lerner would call an "overfunctioner." My perfectionism and quest to swallow the world whole get the better of me, leaving me uncertain, worked up, and in a tizzy. I say yes more than I should, jam-pack my schedule, and forget to budget enough time to recharge my batteries. On top of that, I worry when I feel that I am leaving things unfinished, letting others down, or getting too disorganized. Traces of ADD/ADHD and anxiety are not hard to find in me. My intensity is heightened by my tendencies to feel and think deeply. This intensity is both constructive and destructive, depending on time and place, the flavor of my mood, and the many other factors inevitably tangled into the mix.

Looking back, I can see how some of my most intensive stress episodes involving major losses, chemical imbalances, and overwork shaped the person I am today. Even though each instance brought on a fair share of pain and angst, I also gained a great deal of perspective by working through each of them.

My first trial occurred when I was in the seventh grade. As if adolescence isn't an awkward and bumpy enough developmental phase, I watched my beloved Grandpa Fran reach the pinnacle of suffering from fibrocystic lung disease. All summer, we watched him fight for breath. He passed away three days before school began, and I was absent the entire first week of junior high.

The combination of the immense grief and missing those critical first days of figuring out who to sit with at lunch and how to open my locker in under thirty seconds proved to be a nasty one-two punch for me. I never quite got my bearings and was an easy "geek" target with my bad perm, braces, and string-bean frame. My grades suffered, and so did my self-esteem. Out of step and miserable, I didn't start to feel okay again for at least two years. I have often wondered whether, if my parents and I knew then what we know now, this long stretch of utter sadness could have been alleviated with therapy or other intervention. Luckily, I eventually rebounded—and had learned a lot about grief in the meantime.

My next catastrophe involved loss again—this time unexpected and tragic. My best friend, Margo—neighbor and confidante since age four—was killed with another classmate in a drunk-driving accident just days before our high school graduation. This rocked my world, as you can imagine, and I had no idea how to even begin processing the loss of such a spirited and beautiful friend.

One month later, I underwent ACL surgery for a sports-related tear, which halted my usual teenage comings and goings. Many athletes, especially runners, who stop their sport are at a higher risk for depression because of the sudden drop in their endorphin levels. I spent the summer at home, mostly in bed, stewing in grief and miserable. When I left for college, the adjustment was excruciating since I really had not dealt with Margo's death or accounted for the despair that had crept in.

That's usually how it goes with our mental health. It's not one event but a combination of them that creates such intense brews.

This time, I knew support would make sense. I was bone thin, enduring teeth-gnashing nightmares, and just wasn't *myself.* Getting help proved to be a life-changing decision. I fondly remember Patty, my therapist, who listened as I poured out my heartache and who gave me constructive feedback and the best of her empathy. She also made a great cup of tea and, in fact, sparked my interest in becoming a therapist.

Once I got clearance, I started running and biking again, which also helped recalibrate my system and gave me an extra buffer for dealing with my grief and adjustment issues. Often, we need to take more than one approach to getting the momentum we need to keep pressing forward after we've been walloped.

My next bumps came when I endured extreme postpartum disarray after the births of my daughter and son (three years apart). Like many women, my thyroid became completely thrown off in both instances, sending my mind and body into a plunge like never before. I was the poster person for disaster. My hormones were so awry that I would cry at the drop of a hat, my big goal of the day was getting the mail, and I was at least two hours late everywhere I went. Being the lifelong overachiever, this left me terribly unsettled and questioning my ability to return to functionality. On top of that, as for most new parents, sleep was foreign to me, and just the thought of "one more thing" was enough to overwhelm me. At the time, all bets were off that I'd ever return to adult functioning again. Yikes.

Fortunately, my midwife was astute and realized that something beyond the usual new-parent induction was happening. Sensing that my system was shot, she referred me to a gifted endocrinologist (thyroid doc) who helped get me back up and running. I later learned that symptoms of hypothyroidism (underactive thyroid) mirror nearly all of the signs of depression, and symptoms of hyperthyroidism (overactive thyroid) mimic bipolar/mania, explaining why I felt such a dreadful mix of ups and downs.

This was an incredibly difficult period to endure. Like many new parents, I felt isolated, as though I were going to "lose it," and plain exhausted. Whenever I meet new parents, I have a high level of empathy for them as they are initiated into this new and fundamentally different world. Considering solely the sleep they're not getting and the challenges such exhaustion brings, self-care often ends up going to the very bottom of the list.

As with parenting—or any other major life adjustments, like a new school, job, or relationship—we can quickly be thrown into a tailspin. When losses occur, in particular, our system is likely to go off-kilter. Our bodies and minds are not separate entities. Even if we are "strong willed" or "know it's coming," it can still be incredibly difficult to keep our heads above water when we are dealing with life's whoppers. I learned this in the next "stresscapade" I went through.

That episode occurred while I was investigating stress, coping, and burnout during my doctoral work. I now joke that I was doing my own self-case study. Being the person I am, and given other things going on, I decided that it would be a good idea to maintain the same sense of urgency and intensity with which I typically approach most aspects of my life—so I set a goal to earn my doctorate in under three years. I stuck to aggressive timelines, and with the help of an amazing advisor (thanks, Jane!) and great colleagues, I managed to work up enough juice to keep myself on task. The problem was that the adrenaline was putting my system into overdrive. I was revved up and finding less and less time for self-care. I do not recommend this way of proceeding!

My body didn't love what I was doing. At a routine dental cleaning, my hygienist pointed out that my teeth were showing signs of grinding. I was instructed to wear a night guard to protect them and my jaw from damage. If you Google "teeth grinding," you'll notice that one of the major causes is—yes, you guessed it—stress.[1]

---

[1] In the spirit of self-disclosure, I decided to share my need for a night guard with a few other friends who are of similar molds. I was rather embarrassed

This moment of truth in the dental chair made me reflect. I started to realize the irony (and hypocrisy) of my behavior, and I vowed to ramp up my self care to avoid becoming the epitome of burnout I had set out to investigate. Even though I had little time, I made a point to walk a lot and to do some running, and I found a terrific acupuncturist who helped keep my system in check. I also learned to ask for help (something that most New Englanders are not that accustomed to) and to rely more readily on my friends and family for support. These adjustments, in turn, gave me the momentum to persist and finish in record time. My anxiety had returned to being a motivator and had become less disruptive.

As difficult as these experiences were, I am grateful to have gone through the challenges and pain, for they have shaped my perspective as a person and as a therapist. Stress is indeed a teacher. Some of the wisdom I've learned in and outside of the therapy room has been rather useful:

- Each of us has some version of stress we are dealing with, no matter who we are or where we are from.
- Stress isn't necessarily harmful in the long run. In fact, it can motivate and help us grow.
- High-achieving people are often the hardest on themselves (and sometimes on others).
- Life is a developmental process—we don't magically stop going through stages after surviving adolescence.
- We spend much too time focusing on our weaknesses and not enough on our strengths.
- We are quick to label or judge ourselves/others without looking at context and the many influences affecting behavior.
- People are resilient—the most interesting people are often the ones who have gone through a great deal of pain.
- Even with the best of intentions, it's difficult to follow through with things we know are important, especially in the realm of self-care.

---

until several of them admitted that they also had night guards for the same reason. It looks like daytime stress needs a place to come out at night. Yikes!

- The T-shirt slogan "Running is cheaper than therapy" has a lot of truth in it. The ways in which we take care of (or neglect) our bodies have a direct impact on our mental well-being.
- Most of us are blindsided by what often results from lack of self-care.
- We can't do it alone. We can improve through caring relationships, where we feel supported in learning skills to cope with problems both large and small. Schools and other social institutions play a critical role in this, but not enough resources are devoted to supporting human development and promoting well-being.

Knowing these things makes me feel unsettled, since we are conditioned to focus on competing ways of thinking and priorities that get in the way. Between the crazy-busy pace of life and society's inclination to stigmatize human vulnerability, I wrestle with how to follow through with my own self-care and teach others to do the same.

The critical importance of self-care

It's easy to declare that self-care is crucial but very hard for us to appreciate that truth during difficult times. Just like all of us, I'm a work in progress. Most of us in the field are in it because we "get it," having endured our own variations of stress overload. We're not experts merely because of our training. It's often because we have gone through some real battles ourselves. Also, since we've seen so many unsettling mental health crises happen to well-intentioned, bright, and unsuspecting people, we take self-care seriously, working to be more proactive in what we teach others and live out in our own lives.

> **BOTTOM LINE:** It's important to remember that when we're not continually anchoring ourselves with self-care, it becomes very difficult to make the most of the energy that stress can create.

Self-care involves careful thought and deliberate action in figuring out what drives our thinking and behavior. Left unattended, emotional distress can spiral out of control, and our initial anxiety may rise to a severe level. If there's a weed in the garden and you pull it up, you prevent it from growing. If you leave the weed, it's bound to spread and become more difficult to control. Similarly, a tiny infection in our body is usually treatable—but left completely ignored, the results can be catastrophic. Being *proactive* in any of these circumstances is the way to go.

Avoiding the halt

From the first counseling session I ever provided, to the most recent, a universal theme always presents: people are looking for self-care strategies that *actually* work. They need more than incremental gains—especially when anxiety is sky high. Heavy-duty theory, insider talk, and outdated psychobabble only lead to confusion and more unrest. People need something they can understand *and* follow through on. We get stuck in ruts, lose interest, and get sidetracked. It's the follow-through, or "clinical carryover," that is always the hard part.

Term	Definition	CONSIDER THIS
Clinical carryover	Being able to apply new learning and transfer the momentum generated within a therapeutic session to day-to-day situations.	This is important since it lets us know that strategies are working; therapy can help hold us accountable for needed life changes.

Whether you are in therapy or not, following through with self-care is a real challenge, largely because we often don't have a clear, concrete plan in mind. It's a tall order to actually embrace stress and suffering and find ways to make the most of our circumstances. Besides that, "self-care" is not a widely known concept. We can rattle off the quintessential strategies for *physical* health maintenance: eat right; exercise; hydrate; get enough sleep; stay away from cigarettes and excessive alcohol, and the like. People often put mental and physical health strategies into separate categories, when in fact all of these practices contribute to both aspects of our well-being.

On top of that, knowing what to do to maintain mental health in particular is a bit complex, right? The basic tenets of emotional self-care sometimes stump us. It's the rather complicated stuff like behavioral patterns, personalities, mood fluctuations, communication, and relationships that take effort to decipher. It hasn't been until fairly recently that therapeutic interventions have become less taboo and stigmatized, but we've still got a long way to go. We often don't start paying attention until a severe crisis hits, rather than being proactive and willing to address stress head-on. (We'll unpack this further throughout the book).

Many of us face major time crunches and are over-the-top busy. Life can be an insidiously complex treadmill, with the constant motion leaving us running scared or flat-on-our-back exhausted. It's easy to become derailed, even when setting out to "do the right thing." Our focus can be disrupted when our minds are marinating in anxiety brought on by the inevitable demands of life.

Alcoholics Anonymous and other twelve-step recovery programs have developed some innovative ways to help members keep on track when it comes to self-care. Among a host of great slogans and inspirations are "live and let live," "one day a time," and the Serenity Prayer.

> **BOTTOM LINE:** Many of us know the Serenity Prayer: "God grant me the serenity to accept the things I cannot change, the courage to change the things I can, and the wisdom to know the difference." Several twelve-step groups and other supportive organizations[2] have great slogans that remind us of our need to constantly attend to self-care.

Another classic slogan, though perhaps a less familiar one, is "HALT," standing as a warning against letting yourself get inundated with the feelings of being "Hungry/Angry/Lonely/Tired." This may seem basic, but this mnemonic device can create a sticky structure in our minds, helping us to remember to care for ourselves when we get overwhelmed in the day-to-day grind. As simple as this seems, we benefit from the type of self-inventory and coaching that a framework like HALT provides. These seemingly little things can make a big difference, reminding us of our human vulnerability and encouraging us to keep self-care at the forefront of our minds at all times. We'll talk more about mantras and helpful slogans in the "End Unproductive Thinking" section of the RESET strategies.

What makes follow-through with self-care so complicated? Some of us struggle with finding momentum during moments of life when we are clobbered with illness, loss, or other life circumstances that have depleted us. Over time, motivation and energy feel almost impossible to recover; finding the impetus to meet goals becomes extremely difficult. We want desperately to make changes and invest in self-care, but in these dark zones, we have a hard time mustering up the drive to get back on track and move in a more positive direction.

---

[2]   Check out some examples in the "Recommendations for Further Growth" section in appendix B of this book.

Self-care requires attention and effort!

Even after all these years and with all that I've learned, professionally and personally, I still have to work hard at self-care. It's a constant effort to find effective ways to recalibrate. If it's tricky for someone with the benefit of clinical/stress-management expertise, it's likely to be hard for all of us. The realities of life can creep over any threshold and do a number on us. Just as our cars run out of gas and our batteries run out of power, our emotional reserves dry up and need replenishing. Logic tells us that, in any case, our brains and bodies require attention to function properly. When we take the time to take care of ourselves, we are much more likely to enjoy optimal all-around health.

People who come to see me in therapy often want to know, "Have you ever been depressed?" They sometimes can't picture that the composed person sitting in the chair across from them with degrees on the wall has had her fair share of iffy moments. Appearances can trick us into thinking that everyone else has their act together. But we're all human; and if we neglect to maintain ourselves, it doesn't take much for any of us to get off track.

We benefit from acknowledging the great wonder *and* vulnerability of being human. Suffering is part of life, and our responses are often completely natural and understandable. Yet we often *hate* admitting what we think of as a "weakness"—if we are not as put-together on the inside as we are on the outside. This can be a major barrier to getting needed help. Sometimes we are good at faking it—with the result that others have no idea what we are going through. We are often too ashamed to cry "Uncle!" and get to the drawing board around what we can do differently.

It's so important to have a solid plan that works for more than just a few days, especially given the different directions we get pulled in. We need something to sustain us and help us persevere—something that gets us to put our sneakers on and get moving, to change directions when we're caught in negative thoughts, and to reach out when we're wound up.

Chapter 1 in a Nutshell
The Two Sides of Stress

1. **Where's my reset button?**
   - We look for quick solutions to solve complicated problems.
   - There is rarely an instant fix that solves life's struggles.

2. **The pros and cons of anxiety**
   - The line between natural worry and anxiety is often blurry.
   - It's often challenging to decipher serious warning signs versus everyday stress.
   - Even therapists have teeth-grinding moments and need to practice regular self-care strategies.
   - The same things that drive motivation can, unattended, lead to turmoil.
   - Anxiety is a signal worth listening to, alerting us to danger and threats to well-being.

3. **Avoiding the halt**
   - Self-care helps prevent stress overload.
   - Twelve-step programs show how practical slogans can help us keep self-care front and center.
   - Follow-through to maintain clinical carryover is essential.
   - Today's demands make it hard to maintain optimal mental health.

2

SAVING THE SWIMMER

> Help! I've fallen, and I can't get up!
> —Epic Lifeline commercial

ESSENTIAL QUESTION: What causes you to panic? And when that happens, what helps you regain perspective?

Help, I'm drowning!

"*Help!*" screamed Jack after being tossed into the sea. "*I can't swim!*" Jack Moore* had always been deathly afraid of water and now seemed to be meeting his most feared destiny. His life flashed before his eyes as he desperately cried out for help. He thrashed, bobbed, and swallowed huge gulps of salty water.

There are multiple case examples in the book where pseudonyms are used and identifying details are altered to protect identity and confidentiality. If the story seems familiar, it might just be that we are all human, and the stuff we struggle with is pretty common and "normal," after all! In this book, no real names or identifying information has been used.

In a complete state of panic, Jack overlooked a few critical factors. For one, the water was chest deep. Beside him were rescuers and a flotation device; in front of him, a small island within reach. He had everything needed for survival. For those watching, it bordered on amusing. It wasn't until his anxiety had almost gotten the better of him that he realized he wasn't in as much trouble as he had first thought.

Slowly, Jack's vision cleared, and he grabbed the bobbing lifesaving device at his side. The sounds of his rescuers became audible: "Put your feet down!" Once he touched bottom, Jack was able to notice that the island was surprisingly close. Within a matter of seconds, he had gone from a state of absolute panic to total relief and soon became embarrassed by his seemingly irrational behavior. Still, it wasn't that his fears were totally unwarranted. Would you remain calm if you thought you were drowning?

The fact is, stormy waters can swallow us whole. We all have a "scared swimmer" in us. The trick is figuring out how to be able to see beyond our first instinct to completely panic and to realize that we are much more resourceful than we often realize—and that help may be very close by.

Eustress

Anxiety is a *natural response* to life's zingers. It has a purpose, helping raise adrenaline in sticky situations. Without it, we'd be so laid back that we'd lack the momentum to reach our goals. Athletes know this. Coaches often talk about "eustress," seen as helpful in raising adrenaline needed for performance and endurance.

Term	Definition	CONSIDER THIS
Eustress	Informally known as "good stress," eustress is part of being human; it helps with motivation and performance.	When we realize that "good stress" can be translated into powerful energy, it becomes useful and seems less of a threat to our well-being.

Anxiety can be a motivating force, and even though it can be quite uncomfortable, it can propel us into action. It's been dubbed "the shadow of intelligence"[3] because of its influence in helping us respond to threats and danger. The hard part is working to manage it so that it stays on the constructive side.

Our bodies have the capacity to launch all kinds of hormones, like cortisol, to pump us with the adrenaline rush needed to take action in a given situation. The problem is, when stress is intensive, whether in a given moment or a prolonged period of time, these hormones and signals can throw our systems into a tizzy.

There is a fine line between a healthy level of concern and being overwhelmed. Most conscientious people tend to involve themselves in a lot of mental gymnastics because they care so deeply about the work they are doing, the people they love, or the cause they are supporting. Do you know the drill? In my personal and professional experience, the deep thinkers are the ones who often find themselves saturated with anxiety because of their inclination to overanalyze and worry about *everything*.

What made Jack so consumed that he was unable to see beyond his fears? His anxiety trumped all reason, especially since he felt that his life was at risk. It was easy for him to see that he was not in danger once he came to his senses, but, at the time, he had lost all control. Anxiety has a way of creating blinders and getting smack in the way of rational thinking. Like Jack missing the very obvious cues around him, we can get tunnel vision when struck with our own versions of drowning. We hate being stressed, and so we flounder to get ourselves out of predicaments without slowing down and evaluating how we can work toward healthy resolution.

Bitter lemonade: Anxiety attacks

Some states of anxiety are of such undeniable, epic proportions that they can't be ignored. They remind me of frozen lemonade concentrate without any water—powerfully bitter and a complete sensory overload. If someone offered you a glass, would you drink

---

[3] David Barlow, PhD, asserts that anxiety in threatening situations is quite helpful and even "indispensable." Anxiety, in fact, is needed for survival.

it? Probably not! But, with a bit of water mixed in, it becomes more tolerable and even enjoyable. The concentrate must be diluted to make for the right blend.

Jack's chaotic state mirrors the lemonade concentrate. A perceived threat scares us to the point that we're on the verge of losing serious control. The "water" (reason) hasn't been factored in to make for a "tasty drink" (balanced perspective), and we're stuck with a bitter blend of emotion. We'll cover how to combat this in the "Realize" chapter.

Blended Lemonade and Balanced Perspective are Less Bitter

Anxiety attacks are like an "internal blush"—they can wash over us faster than a face can turn red, producing a range of frightening sensations like not being able to breathe, swallow, or slow our pulse. Emergency room workers regularly see people who have come in thinking that they were having a heart attack only to discover that the symptoms were brought on by stress. The symptoms are so similar that the natural conclusion is "I'm going to die!" Sometimes panic attacks are so invasive that they lead to scary, in-the-moment thoughts like "I've gone crazy!" or "This is *never* going to go away!"

If you've ever had a panic attack, you know how utterly consuming they are. They happen like an instant tidal wave crashing over the walls of our physical and mental systems. It's nearly impossible in that moment for anyone to talk sense into you. And, like Jack, we later see some of our irrationality—but this realization may not prevent the same thing from happening again. These moments lead to a serious aversion to stress, to say the least! We tend to lump all stress into the "bad" category without realizing that it can actually help us grow and develop character, grit, and resilience.

Is this normal?

It's important to note that not everyone who has ever had a panic attack has a clinically significant problem with anxiety. In fact, most people experience at least a few in their lifetime.

Persistent panic attacks. Persistent panic attacks, on the other hand, can be categorized on the moderate-to-severe side of anxiety, depending on their intensity, frequency, and the circumstances—known as "psychosocial stressors"[4]—a person is facing. These stressors have a huge impact on our thoughts, feelings, and well-being. They are often tied to the onset of anxiety and depression and tend to be connected with a wide range of situations, like death, divorce, unemployment, academic problems, and more.

Term	Definition	CONSIDER THIS
Psychosocial stressor	An unsettling event or circumstance within your social environment that affects your well-being; can include lack of support system, financial worry, unemployment, or rocky relationships.	It's extremely important to remember the context you find yourself in and to factor this into your self-care plan; we often judge ourselves too harshly without fully accounting for what's happening to or around us.

---

[4] The American Psychological Association's DSM-5, the bible of mental health diagnosis, provides a thorough depiction of what is known as "Axis IV" environmental factors that impact diagnosis, treatment, and prognosis.

> **BOTTOM LINE:** When we notice the amount of our psychosocial stressors going up, it's important to step up our self-care to help counteract the anxiety we are likely to experience. If we practice self-care regularly, we will be better grounded during periods of our lives when there is upheaval.

Rumination. When we are in the throes of stress, we can have all kinds of responses. Anxieties falling on the mild-to-moderate level on the stress spectrum are what I call "treadmill" types, ones that leave us in a constant state of unrest. The "what ifs" invade our thought processes, leading to distraction and exhaustion. Clinically, we call this "rumination," leading to a state of "I just can't get my mind to stop."

Those who ruminate are "overthinkers" who run through their thoughts over and over while remaining in the same overstimulated mental state. Treadmill types of anxiety are often hidden, making for an agonizing situation for those enduring it. Most are unlikely to recognize what is happening and even less apt to get help for it. When fears are kept hidden, they can often become more problematic since the worry takes on a life of its own. The mind churns, repeating the same line of thinking without ever arriving at a new destination or more clarity.

Dr. Nolen-Hoeksema, a renowned psychologist from Stanford University, spent her career examining the impact of this tendency. She put it as follows: "When there is any pause in our daily activities many of us are flooded with worries, thoughts, and emotions that swirl out of control, sucking our emotions and energy down, down, down ... we are suffering from an epidemic of overthinking."[5]

---

[5] Dr. Susan Kay Nolen-Hoeksema, psychologist extraordanaire, penned *Women Who Think Too Much: How to Break Free of Overthinking and Reclaim Your Life.* Her practical insights on avoiding the disruption that comes with the constant treadmill of ruminating thoughts are golden.

Over time, this anxiety treadmill takes a major toll on well-being. Our minds want to work hard, and they will—unfortunately, when we attach ourselves to stressful thoughts, such mental activity is just not productive. In fact, a huge portion of time and energy is often devoted to worrying over things that may never occur (Jack's fear that he was drowning) or cannot be changed, anyway. What a waste.

Term	Definition	CONSIDER THIS
Thought rumination	A way of thinking that involves intensive analysis of certain thoughts and feelings. When this repeated revisiting occurs, it leaves us stirred up, consumed, and stuck.	Ruminating can ensnare us in a seemingly never-ending trap. This can interfere with more productive thinking and activity. When our emotions run high, we have a tendency to become embroiled in such a pattern.

Thought rumination can be so disruptive that it shows up on symptom checklists for bipolar depression and is often associated with this diagnosis. However, even stress and anxiety can provoke rumination, with some people more prone to it because of varying factors, such as personality, social conditioning, and intellectual depth. Lots of times, it's the brightest among us who tend to overthink and dissect everything. When our minds are not engaged in enough learning or in productive pursuits, they may go into a kind of distressing overdrive.

Rumination is not necessarily enough to constitute diagnosis of a major psychological problem, but the obsessive nature of it can still do a number. John Ratey, a dynamic Harvard psychiatrist, is one of the most prolific writers about what he calls "shadow syndromes."[6] People with shadow syndromes tend to have three or four of the ten or so symptoms that would indicate that they have a clinically significant diagnosis. In short, they have a mild form of something serious.

So, here's the catch: It's the people falling right under the threshold of mental health diagnoses who pay a high price, since their problem often goes undetected and untreated. They can hold it together outside of the home, while in the meantime they—those in the shadows—(along with their loved ones) can really be held hostage to the symptoms they experience.

> **BOTTOM LINE:** If you're dealing with even a few "mild" symptoms of anxiety, they can still wreak havoc. While the tendency is to try to hide or dismiss what we are enduring, it's wise to address these symptoms before they take on a life of their own.

"Self-awareness hell." Take Janis Bates, for example. She is a classic ruminator, even though this fact remains undetectable to most. Make no mistake, her self-sabotage is high ranking.

Janis's story
Janis lives in the past and the future—always thinking of every possible contingency of what could have happened or that may lay ahead *and* spending huge amounts of time second-guessing herself. She dissects every conversation she's had and finds a way to beat herself up over decisions she has made. Those in her close circles sense that something is wrong, but it's disguised enough that no one is pressing her to get some much-needed help.

Janis feels inadequate and insecure and wants nothing more than for people to like her. She feels pressure to "be all" and "do all" in her relationships, expecting way more of herself than anyone in her life would ever dream of asking

---

[6]   John Ratey's work brilliantly shatters misconceptions and speaks to the most pertinent issues of our times.

from her. Her relationships have become performance based, leaving her perpetually worried that she has let someone down when she hasn't lived up to the unrealistic expectations she thinks others will hold her to.

When things go wrong, Janis plays them over and over again in her head and has trouble moving forward. She spends hours ruminating over everything, even her own anxiety levels. This distracts her from being happy with the many things that are actually going *well* in her life. This became a daily occurrence, evolving from a pattern that began very early on in her development. Janis calls this "self-awareness hell."

Why does she torment herself in this manner? Worry rents all the space in her head that could otherwise be devoted to much more productive activity, like creative brainstorming, goal setting, and problem solving. Janis designates the majority of thinking time unproductively; as a result, she's completely worn out. Not only that, but all her focus on what's not working well reinforces her insecurity, leading to the classic self-fulfilling prophecy: her anxiety-based ruminations have undermined her work and relationships—thus causing her to fulfill her own "prophecy" about failure.

Like panic attacks, this type of anxiety is quite paralyzing. Both forms leave us stuck and depleted of energy. This version of anxiety goes hand in hand with depression. The anxiety sucks the lifeblood out, leaving us too deflated and too tired to break the cycle. Talk about despair.

Mallory's story

For a while, Mallory Bingham was able to manage the constant demands she faced with relative ease, but lately, she finds herself swamped. She deals with what she calls "nonstop chitter chatter" in her mind, always jumping from thought to thought and juggling what feels like an overwhelming number of tasks. She feels constantly revved up with a sense of urgency to "hurry" because there's so much to do. She sometimes catches herself racing around in a near panic, even when she is not necessarily in a rush.

We could liken this form of anxiety to a "pinball machine," with the ball's being constantly flung from one point to another.

Before she had kids, Mallory was fairly organized and managed to make her way through college without event. Now, she is consumed with the details of orchestrating three busy children and keeping her consulting work afloat. Her husband, Thom, is overwhelmed with the pressures of running his growing business, and although they work well as a team, there isn't enough downtime to even decide what changes in their routines may tip the balance and make life a little less stressful.

Mallory finds it hard to relax and slow her mind down, especially at night. The lack of sleep is not helping—she is irritable and snaps at her family way more than she would like. She feels guilty and defective since so many of her friends seem to "have it together." Mallory is caught in a cycle of anxiety-based adrenaline rushes and complete exhaustion. She feels frantic, then flat—*over and over* again.

Mallory forgets to account for the fact that the early parenting years leave very little time for self-care. She blames herself for shortcomings that have a lot more to do with circumstance than personal flaws. The season of life she finds herself in tends to be demanding and exhausting.[7] When a cluster of circumstances affect the amount of sleep, workout, or alone time we have, our ability to cope can be compromised, similar to when our immune system is run down, leading to higher susceptibility to getting worn out and sick.

Phobias. Some anxieties take on the form of phobias, with very specific triggers, such as fear of heights, fire, bugs, elevators, car rides, and crowds. Intrusive thoughts are another form of anxiety,

---

[7] Parents are notorious for working around the clock—with taking care of children as the "second shift." Further, a "third shift" involves maintaining relationships and keeping up with social traditions (and obligations)—like birthdays, baby showers, holidays, anniversaries, and more, which have traditionally fallen into the laps of women. These tasks can be time consuming and eat up any chances of "free" time to decompress.

blindsiding us with disruptive and frightening inferences. They are likely to arise in the face of severe psychosocial stressors and life changes, especially if one has a genetic disposition toward anxiety. They lead to fears of involuntarily doing something impulsive and disastrous. These intrusions lead to such thoughts as "I'm afraid I'm going to jump out of this car" or "What if I make a fool of myself in front of everyone?"

Kate's story

This was the case for Kate Powers, who was dealing with a highly secret, toxic phobia that left her head spinning. Her drive and determination have always epitomized perfectionism, and she refers to herself as "methodical" and "type-A all the way." Ambitious to the core, Kate broke through the glass ceiling to become the youngest and first female CEO of a large metropolitan company. Poised and savvy, she soared in every aspect of her professional life. Kate became used to success and was formulaic in how she approached tasks, meeting rigorous goals and standards. She rarely flinched, even under intense pressure. Her colleagues called her "a force to be reckoned with," and she was respected and revered because of her tenacity.

At thirty, Kate was introduced to a battle with unimaginable anxiety after the birth of her daughter. Postpartum depression receives a lot of attention, but its wicked cousin, postpartum anxiety, is one of the worst uninvited guests imaginable. Lots of women experience their chemistry going so awry that they are flooded with intrusive fears, thoughts, and panic symptoms, compounding the already-difficult adjustment to motherhood.

Frightening and debilitating postpartum anxiety, like postpartum depression, comes on without warning, and to say Kate was distraught would be an understatement. It was like someone had tripped a switch in her; she became obsessed with the thought that her house was going to burn down. Upon leaving home, Kate couldn't fight the overwhelming impulse to check and make sure the stove was turned off. Often, she'd leave home, only to have to rush back, in a state of panic, to ensure it was shut off. She constantly sent frantic texts to her husband; inevitably, he always discovered that, indeed, the stove was already off.

Kate tried to flex every ounce of intellectual muscle she had to overcome her irrationality. No amount of sheer will was enough. She finally sought support from her nurse practitioner, who guided her toward her recovery process. Apparently, her hormones had been thrown off and she was experiencing a textbook—and very treatable—version of postpartum anxiety. She was surprised to learn how common this syndrome is, having heard only of the closely related, infamous postpartum depression.

Many women experience panic symptoms and have what are known as "checking" behaviors upon becoming new mothers. Many find themselves checking to make sure the baby is breathing, that appliances are unplugged, and that there aren't any lurking dangers. These instincts are useful and helpful, but when they become too intense, they can be disruptive. Kate was greatly relieved that a very mild "as-needed" antianxiety medication,[8] along with some supportive therapy, yoga classes, and time with other new parents, was enough to help put her back on track. She was grateful to finally be able to embrace motherhood with less trepidation, without being saturated with constant bothersome thoughts and feelings. She felt less alone and more secure as time went on and was thrilled to be back on course after experiencing such tremendous uncertainty and disruption.

Obsessive thinking. Another form of unruly anxiety that quickly sabotages the quality of life for everyone in its path is known as *obsessive thinking*. Not only does the person experiencing it suffer directly, but

---

[8]   Sometimes daily medications are needed to treat anxiety, but often what is known as a "PRN," the medical community's lingo for "as needed," can help the body recalibrate. Like most medical terms, it comes from the Latin *pro re nata* means "when necessary." Asking your doctor/practitioner is the first step in deciding what's best for you. In general, medications should be used sparingly and as a last resort in most circumstances. More on that soon.

those around them also are deeply impacted. Doug Harris's wife, Sahara, can verify that.

Doug and Sahara's story

Doug had a weak stomach for anything medical. He began worrying more about his health than he did about taking care of himself. In his midtwenties, he developed some intense fears around going to the doctor, even though he was wildly afraid that he would get sick. At this time, Doug had started to put on weight and wasn't getting nearly the amount of exercise he had throughout his life as an avid tennis player. He entered graduate school and was under a great deal of pressure. A bout with bronchitis sidelined him for twelve days. He had trouble breathing, and he was overwhelmed by these frightening symptoms of the illness. Soon after, Doug noticed that he couldn't stop worrying about getting sick again. As much as he tried, he was haunted by intrusive thoughts and images of devastating illness. He found himself searching online to make sense of his "mystery" ailments that convinced him that he was dying—only to discover, when he checked with his doctor, that he was perfectly fine.

Sahara joked that he was becoming a hypochondriac, and he was even able to laugh with her when he wasn't in his obsessive-thought mode. When the pendulum swung back, it knocked him out every time. He began losing sleep, and his heart seemed to be beating out of his chest. Doug kept it under control at work, but his colleagues were worried about the dark circles under his eyes and his distractibility. At home, Doug became withdrawn and irritable. He barely spoke to Sahara, but when he did, he was curt and cynical.

Sahara tried to diffuse the situation with humor, but the truth was that she was fed up. It was hard for her to understand why he couldn't just "snap out of it," and she was tired of spending hours trying to talk some sense into him. Sahara began spending extra time at work to avoid Doug's rants. She befriended a coworker, Gerardo, who surprisingly was dealing with a similar situation with his wife, Nina. Over time, the boundaries of their work relationship blurred, and

Sahara began feeling a magnetic attraction to Gerardo. She became frightened when she recognized that she was right on the cusp of an emotional affair.

Scared by the prospect of losing Doug, she urged him to seek treatment. Reluctantly, he phoned a clinical social worker specializing in cognitive-behavioral treatment, and over long months, began having breakthroughs. Both Doug and Sahara were relieved that his anxiety was no longer holding them hostage. Rather than facing off against each other, they began working together proactively to address what had become a serious interference to their happiness. Life wasn't perfect, but as Doug's anxiety was managed, they were both able to grow as individuals and as a couple.

Obsessive thinking and phobias tend to have a high consequence, leaving us marinating in worry. Many times, they can be hidden, since triggers like heights, bugs, or snakes can often be avoided. Other times, internal phobias are more difficult to avoid since they relate to fears associated with our health, finances, social relationships, and other unavoidable issues.

While Doug's anxiety levels were a detriment to his relationship, he was able to get treatment and move forward, largely because of Sahara's prompting. She was a powerful force in helping him to recover. Doug and Sahara also had a strong network of friends and family supportive of them, which proved extremely beneficial.

Impact on relationships
Unfortunately, for some people, healthy relationships become totally out of reach because of anxiety, further complicating their chances of recovery. Such high anxiety levels can disrupt development and maintenance of relationships, compromising satisfaction, intimacy, and happiness. Anxiety gets in the way, and unless we are aware of what is happening, we are more likely to live in an isolated fashion, only to stew further in a sea of self-depreciation and stress.

When experiencing high levels of anxiety, it is not uncommon to stay away from people and situations that may take the lid off. Todd Pitman was in this boat. Over the years, he became less and less involved with friends and his family. Despite some obvious peculiarities, they chalked it up to his personality quirks. They had little idea how much he suffered.

Todd's story

From an early age, Todd was clearly gifted. His hallmark high IQ and drive were something to swoon over. As an adult, he had become extremely accomplished as a lawyer, earning well over $350,000 annually. Single and under forty, he sat on a whopping nest egg. Pressured by family, he succumbed and bought a large house to satisfy their white-picket-fence dreams for him. Plus, they didn't know the full extent of the secret he was keeping.

Todd was struggling with severe obsessive-compulsive disorder (OCD), with precise cleaning rituals that would put my "cleanliness is next-to-godliness" mother-in-law to shame! His routines were so scripted that any deviation would throw him into upheaval, and he'd have to start all over. White-knuckled and heart racing, he devoted hours each day to try to squelch the overwhelming obsessive thinking that was flooding his brain.

While Todd's schedule was intense, he truly found satisfaction at work. Plus, he was able to put his OCD tendencies to good use there, applying his obsessive attention to detail to every case. His colleagues marveled at his acumen. Outside the office, it was a different story. Todd was becoming a prisoner in his own head and home. His severe germ phobia had taken a turn for the worse. He'd gone about managing it in his old apartment, but the new house was exhausting him. When he arrived home each night, he stripped down to his boxers before even walking through the door. He was spending hours scrubbing every inch of his home because of his fears of contamination. Todd tried to avoid most areas of the house, since if he made even remote contact with any surface, it caused him to spiral into a cleaning frenzy to reset the damage he thought he had done. Each night, he collapsed on the floor to watch some television, unable to bring himself to sit or lie on his expensive furniture so he wouldn't have to clean it afterward.

Term	Definition	Consider This
Obsessive-compulsive disorder[9]	An interference characterized by high anxiety and intrusive thoughts producing fear and worry. These unwanted thoughts can lead to behavior that may temporarily allow relief but resurface again when triggered.	Generally, people recognize that their behavior is extreme, but the anxiety overrides rhyme or reason. This is more serious than everyday anxiety— it's best to seek professional support.

The final straw for Todd was an unexpected visit from a group of friends. He was barely able to enjoy their company, and once they left he stayed up all night "decontaminating" the entire premises. The next day, the demands of the case he had invested countless hours in became too much for his tired brain. He overlooked an important filing deadline, leaving his colleagues outraged and perplexed by his mistake.

Todd's struggle with OCD[10] was extremely disruptive to his emotional well-being. His social life suffered greatly, and his isolation continued to increase. His friends became perturbed about his reluctance to invite them over, and he had little time to meet up with them because of the amount of time he was taking to clean his home.

---

[9] Check out http://www.nimh.nih.gov/ to learn more about OCD symptoms and treatment approaches.

[10] Jonathan B. Grayson, PhD, is cofounder of the Anxiety and OCD Treatment Center of Philadelphia and an assistant clinical professor of psychiatry at Temple University Medical School. Check out his *Freedom from Obsessive-Compulsive Disorder: A Personalized Recovery Program for Living with Uncertainty* for some useful perspective and strategies.

Todd's treatment road was rocky. He began with a combined approach of cognitive-behavioral treatment along with a low dosage of antianxiety medication. He put his home up for sale to avoid further functional decline. While some improvements were made, Todd's prognosis was compromised due in part to the severity of his symptoms and length of time (seven years) he waited before getting treatment. He often reflected that he should not have let his OCD reach such a heightened level, regretting that he had missed out on so much.

While Todd's example is unsettling, many others struggle in less extreme ways that nonetheless profoundly affect their relationships. This was Brendon Martel to a tee.

Brendon's story

Brendon was on top of the world in high school. Poised and popular, he had a robust social life with lots of dates. He went on to earn a four-year degree and, like so many college graduates, took a job in retail while he waited for something more in line with his career aspirations. Mature for his age, he had difficulty finding a partner he could relate to. He considered most people he met as superficial and began to worry that he would "never find someone."

This line of thinking intensified, and Brendon began freezing up in social situations. He stammered over his words and felt increasingly awkward. Brendon's blunders were not nearly as disastrous as he magnified them to be in his own mind. Gone were the days when he could easily shake things off. He was in a game of pickle within his own head, which, as you can imagine, was no picnic.

Following a few unpleasant encounters, Brendon decided that staying home was the best remedy. After a few months of this "social sabbatical," he lost his nerve completely and was extremely uncomfortable in his interactions. He wondered if he would ever regain the courage to get "back in the mix" and feel less insecure. His confidence was at an all-time low, and his anxiety was mounting. Brendon had spent way too much time analyzing himself and was convinced that he would never get out of this pattern.

The clincher for Brendon was at his brother's wedding. Feeling down, he drank an exorbitant amount of alcohol, and down came the dominoes. He instigated a major fight that led to a reality TV–type scene at the end of the reception.

The next day, full of shame, he came unwound with his family, causing them great concern, since they had never seen that side of him. Brendon's aunt was a savvy therapist; she helped him find a licensed clinical social worker, and he sheepishly started the process of getting support.

Within a few months, Brendon's confidence began to increase, and his worry became more manageable. Over time, he started networking and getting back into the social groove. He had learned a great deal about himself and was able to better see his strengths and be less self-critical. Brendon vowed that he would make a concerted effort to invest in his emotional health to prevent returning to the dark place he had found himself in. With all he had been through, self-care had now become a huge priority.

> **Bottom Line:** Letting anxiety fester can lead to an emotional boiling point. It's wise to be proactive and avoid coming too close to the edge.

The world we live in

Even when we don't have a major propensity toward panic or treadmill-style anxiety, we can find ourselves simply stuck because of the sheer nature of life today. Things like fiscal cliffs, skyrocketing costs, violence, poverty, and war leave us reeling, uncertain, and worried. Our panicked reactions are, indeed, natural responses to much of what we see in the world around us.

We also live in a context where we're bombarded with commercial messages and pressure to have picture-perfect bodies,[11] homes, and

---

[11] An incredible illustration of the power and negative impact of the media is in Jennifer Siebel Newsom's documentary, *Miss Representation*. See www. Missrepresentation.org to find out how to view this compelling account.

cars. Things like the latest upgrade, pedicures, braces, and Pinterest-inspired birthday parties would have been considered luxuries in the past, and still are for many of us.

Years ago, it would have been unheard of to have a brand-new car, wardrobe, or the types of vacations that many families of today take for granted. Many privileged Americans suffer from what my teenagers call "first-world pains"—"problems" like not having enough dip with your chips or having a vacation spoiled by bad weather. The glitz of the "good life" often spoils our perspective, creating a great deal of stress and dissatisfaction, even when there's so much to be grateful for.

> **BOTTOM LINE:** Living in a culture where commercialism blasts us, contentment is hard to come by. The standards have become so inflated that many feel unsatisfied and "less than" if they don't have the latest and greatest. The shaky economic climate adds fuel to the fire, leaving us scrambling to reinvent ourselves and find jobs, housing, colleges, and all the "stuff" we have been conditioned to think we need.[12] Talk about anxiety provoking!

Today's generation Y has incredible opportunities, yet there is a price to pay for such privilege. College education has become widely available, creating enormous opportunities for and, in some cases, pressures on today's students, with skyrocketing competition and costs. Increasing global competition and dismal market conditions are leaving many with limited prospects. These factors contribute to heightened anxiety for all people trying to find their way and make a sustainable living.

---

[12]   The Center for a New American Dream has published some persuasive examples. See www.newdream.org for more, or check out How Much Is Enough? by Robert and Edward Skidelsky.

In many sections of the United States[13] and across the world, such luxuries are not commonplace,[14] and many struggle to survive and secure basic needs. Poverty creates devastating conditions that lead to terrible outcomes for far too many. Poverty is severely threatening the well-being of children and families across the world. When we're tempted to want more "things," consider the ramifications of not having drinking water, a safe neighborhood, or decent food. If you have these things, they are luxuries to be appreciated. If you do not, part of your self-care will be survival focused and will include the search for people and resources to help you.

When basic needs are unmet, it becomes extremely challenging to make gains emotionally and psychologically. A classic example of this in psychology is seen in Maslow's hierarchy of needs. This nifty triangle has a lot to teach us about our social, emotional, and physical needs as humans.

Maslow's Hierarchy of Needs

---

[13] The United States is facing unprecedented disparities: http://stateofworkingamerica.org/.

[14] Imagine if the world were a village of a hundred people—here's a glimpse of what it would look like: http://www.youtube.com/watch?v=r6eTr4ldDYg. Talk about perspective.

> **Bottom Line:** Besides the 1 percent, who in the world doesn't have some degree of financial concern in today's economy? Financial instability and poverty are directly connected to our emotional well-being. The disparities in our world are astounding, and "the market" leaves many with rising debt and severe financial strain.

❧

In this chapter, you've met Jack Moore, Janis Bates, Mallory Bingham, Kate Powers, Doug Harris, Todd Pitman, and Brendon Martel. They've all had significant difficulties to overcome—like ruminating thoughts, low confidence, compulsive behavior, broken relationships, and varying degrees of anxiety. Meanwhile, they each have their share of resources at hand—friends, caring practitioners, new insights, high levels of passion, conscientiousness, and drive.

Our strengths, when not operating in optimal circumstances or moving in a direction that makes for positive momentum, can lead to difficulties. In many instances, strengths and weaknesses are closely linked. Our most pronounced characteristics are the very things that make us either *succeed* or *struggle*. We're better equipped to make the most of our stress when we realize the integral connection between our strengths and weaknesses. The qualities that drove Todd Pitman to unrest at home were the very ones that led to great accomplishments at work. Certain factors can bring out the worst in us—even when it comes to our best traits. This is natural. Think of wind, rain, and fire. They can caress or destroy, depending on their level of intensity.

Strengths and Weaknesses are Intricately Linked

Pay attention!

Remember Jack Moore, our swimmer? Anxiety is like the salt in Jack's eyes, getting in the way of seeing beyond the immediate. For each of us, our ability to stay above the surface and make it to shore is impacted by the different conditions we find ourselves in, combined with our thresholds at the moment. Some of us swim in shark-infested waters; others are pinched by annoying crabs. At times, the water temperature is unbelievably cold, and the distance to the rescue boat seems dreadfully far. Sometimes we have large weights chained around us, and other times it's just hard tolerating the sea salt. Some of us happen to be Phelps-ishly built for swimming, and some of us sink despite our best efforts.

Regardless of the conditions or our natural tolerance of the elements, part of managing life is to keep treading water in hopes of making it back to solid ground again. Repeatedly panicking when the conditions are rough is likely to perpetuate a long and dismal cycle of anxiety and disarray. It's easy to get caught up in a pattern of distress and overlook the fact that trying something different might actually do the trick.

Since seventh grade, I've worn contact lenses. To remedy my red morning eyes that have come over time, I began using eyedrops ritualistically, only to find that the more I used them, the redder my eyes became. Ironically, I was inadvertently making worse the very thing I was trying to fix! This is so often the case when we grab onto habitual or conventional approaches to managing life's demands. Einstein defined insanity as doing the same thing over and over again and expecting different results.[15] We cannot expect to *feel* well and *be* well without creating and following a different plan—one that will deliver positive results.

It's crucial to notice when—as happens too often—the beliefs, behaviors, and relationships we are involved in end up being counterproductive to our well-being. We waste a tremendous amount of time and energy in panic mode, mulling things over and torturing ourselves (and sometimes those around us). Being able to change these

---

[15] That Einstein sure was a genius, no?

patterns is a beginning step in being more settled and happier. What might you need to readjust along these lines?

> **Bottom Line:** Start paying attention to your anxiety levels and how you are responding. It's a process worth investing in. By doing so, you will be better equipped to manage the conditions you find yourself in. Stress can either motivate us or disrupt our self-care.

Dissect and Reflect

Of the different versions of anxiety in this chapter, I most relate to:

Knowing this, I plan to do the following three things to try to feel more at ease:
1)
2)
3)

Suggested activity: Google "SWOT analysis" and follow the steps to complete one. Once finished, ask yourself:

1) What strengths are most pronounced?
2) Can I see any linkages and connections with any identified weaknesses?
3) As a result of completing the SWOT, what have I learned?
4) How will I use this moving forward?

Chapter 2 in a Nutshell
Saving the Swimmer

1. **Help! I'm drowning!**
   - There's a "scared swimmer" in all of us.
   - Eustress can help us deal with life's curveballs.

2. **Bitter lemonade**
   - Jack Moore lost sight of his resources when in a full-blown panic.
   - Anxiety is like bitter lemonade concentrate without the needed blend of water to taper its intensity.
   - Psychological stressors impact our well-being and ability to reason.

3. **Is this normal?**
   - Jack, Janis, Mallory, Kate, Doug, Todd, and Brendon all had something important to teach us about the insidious carousel of anxiety.
   - Thought rumination is a force to be reckoned with and happens outside the radar of diagnosis, wreaking havoc for those in the "shadows."
   - When financial stability or basic needs aren't met, our health and well-being are compromised, and we're likely to show signs of distress.
   - Our most pronounced characteristics can be either a great help or hindrance, depending on the level of intensity and the circumstances we find ourselves in.

4. **Pay attention!**
   - The process of evaluating our patterns can lead to healthier connections, actions, behaviors, and increased happiness.
   - Don't keep dumping the eyedrops in! Work to identify what other strategies will be more effective over the long haul.

3

Therapy 101

Owning our story can be hard but not nearly as difficult
as spending our lives running from it.
—Brené Brown

Essential Question: What strategies are
you relying on to manage your self-care?

What works?

I've always prided myself on being a competent therapist. People
seem to like me, I usually have a waiting list, and it seems like people
improve after a few sessions.

Even though I'm tempted to believe it, it's hardly my charm, clanky
earthy garb, sunk-in chocolate-colored suede couch, or even my costly
clinical training that helps me entirely.

Along the way, I've realized that people need more than all of the
proverbial nods and oohs and aahs of an attentive therapist. They
need something practical they can *do* to deal with what's on their
plate. People need something tangible. Something to rely on between
the fifty-minute-every-other-week sessions. Something that works.
Something immediate. Because most of us have pretty full plates.

This hit me especially hard on a certain rainy New England Monday. The backdrop was particularly fitting as I met with Meg Meany, who was saturated with anxiety.

Meg had every reason to be losing hair. And she was. She showed me two quarter-sized bald spots on the top and side of her scalp, indicating that she had alopecia areata.[16] To say that she was highly stressed would be a gross understatement. Between her fiery toddler, unruly teen, disinterested husband, lack of money, and challenging past, she was at her wit's end. Like many others facing tough problems, she needed intervention—fast.

It wasn't Meg's first shot at therapy. She'd had several go-arounds and had made real strides. She was a trooper in many ways. Now, in addition to a nail-biting past, Meg was dealing with a heaping dose of family and money problems. In the middle of it all, she had invested nearly zero time in her emotional and physical well-being. Now the stress was crashing over her from head to toe, with bald spots as glaring representations of her complete and utter overload.

As you can imagine, it didn't take long to determine that Meg was coming from a place of total self-neglect. Not only was she working seventy-plus hours weekly, but she was eating junk, barely sleeping, and fresh air was virtually a foreign concept to her. Even worse, she couldn't find time to exercise, she and her husband had lost all forms of intimacy, she felt sick constantly, and she rarely saw any of her friends or involved herself in her community—all things that would be considered "protective factors" by experts in resilience.[17] Her hair loss was the clincher that prompted her to dial my number.

---

[16] In addition, stress can cause such conditions as telogen effluvium and trichotillomania. They are as awful to deal with as they sound. Check out the work of Daniel K. Hall-Flavin at the Mayo Clinic for more discussion. I've seen a lot of people arrive into therapy when this happens. I don't recommend waiting until reaching that point.

[17] Resilience is getting a ton of attention these days, as we think about our military veterans experiencing PTSD and about children who have been traumatized. The conversation is vital for well-being and restoration and deserves to be front and center when we consider the best-known ways to prevent and treat stress overload.

Sound like fun?

The truth is, Meg is not alone. Stress can seriously zap momentum, leaving us barely able to follow through with the basics. We get furiously busy, consumed, and sidetracked. I've worked with people from all walks of life—rich and poor, young and old, blue collar and white collar, and every variation in between. I've had lengthy conversations with parents, teachers, nurses, doctors, managers, clergy, and other therapists who are stressed to the max, running on fumes, and on the verge of burnout.

Term	Definition	Consider This
Protective factor	Something that prevents or reduces vulnerability to distress, such as a strong social support system or relying on healthy coping strategies and skills.	There are many paths to reducing stress and its impact, both within the mind/body/spirit and in our surrounding environment. Look for them!

Bottom Line: Things like faith, humor, family, and the presence of caring people in our lives have all been shown to be "protective factors" or "developmental assets,"[18] even in dire circumstances when there are many obstacles. Remember, we keep developing throughout our lives, so being cognizant of what helps us to keep growing and improving is important.

---

[18] The Search Institute's listing of adolescents' internal and external protective traits is worth peeking at, with many items relevant to teens and adults alike: http://www.search-institute.org/research

Jamie's story

Recently, Jamie Wang stepped through my door, and his anxiety was palpable. His own worst critic, he had spent most of his life in a constant state of worry and self-sabotage. After a few minutes, he had laid out what had proven to be his own recipe for disaster:

- four hours of nightly sleep
- three daily meals (if he was lucky ... with "meals" loosely defined and completely devoid of nutrition)
- two jobs
- one rocky marriage
- zero exercise

Throw in dashes of alcohol, tons of coffee, creeping debt, and no support system—equaling a severely wound-up Jamie. He could barely sit still, jumped from one thought to the next, and his big dreams and plans seemed unsustainable given the way he was neglecting the basics. Eventually, Jamie learned to start taking care of himself and was pleasantly surprised at the differences he quickly noticed.

BOTTOM LINE: Putting a depressant into your system may relax you for a bit, but not if you're prone to abuse. If you're drinking too much, your body is trying to reset and find relief. This may be a cue that you need to take a closer look at. Quenching your thirst for relaxation with that delightful glass of red wine or cold beer may serve you well in moderation, but approaching this very carefully is prudent, given the high number of people who can't have "just one."

Staying the course

Does any of this sound familiar? What does your recipe consist of? What are you consuming (or not consuming) that add up to your bottom line? Be honest with yourself. Here's a beginning checklist to consider:

Ingredient	Ask yourself
Pleasure	Do I laugh a lot? Have I stopped doing things I once felt were enjoyable? Do I take myself too seriously?
Sleep	What is my sleep pattern? How much do I get on average? Do I feel rested?
Exercise	Do I move? Am I regularly working up a sweat? Do I feel healthy and in shape?
Food/beverage intake	What am I putting into my body? Is there too much or too little of something in my diet?[19] Am I hydrated? How much caffeine and alcohol[20] do I consume?
Connections	Do I have a support system? If I'm struggling, who can I turn to? Do I participate in activities outside of work or immediate family? Do my associates lift me up?

---

[19] The good old food pyramid has been replaced ... move over bacon, there's something leaner! Check out http://www.choosemyplate.gov/.

[20] Centers for Disease Control and Prevention (CDC), Alcohol-Related *Disease Impact (ARDI). Atlanta: CDC. Check out the CDC's* take on this at http://www.cdc.gov/alcohol/fact-sheets/alcohol-use.htm.

Setting boundaries	Are most of my relationships mutual, or do I tend to be the one giving most of the time? Do I feel stretched by pressures to do for everyone else? Do I feel guilty or have trouble saying no?
Faith	Do I live true to my convictions and beliefs? Do I spend time nurturing and growing my spiritual side? Am I living for a purpose beyond myself?

You can see this isn't rocket science, yet it's easy to overlook. Why is follow-through so challenging? We get swept away and completely neglect these basics—yet I could have a field day telling you all the neurophysiologic, health, psychological, social, and spiritual benefits of attending to them. How do we forget these simple things?

Thousands of books and articles exist on each individual element in the table above, and if you look at any stress-management tips, these basics are sure to play the most prominent role. These are not novel concepts. Why do we neglect to keep good personal care routines? I'm a stress "expert," but I even buckle under pressure and start resorting to archaic habits. It's so easy to derail.

I've always had a fascination with the biblical verse "I don't really understand myself, for I want to do what is right, but I don't do it. Instead, I do what I hate."[21] That about nails it, doesn't it? I'd be rich if I had a dollar for every time I heard someone tell me that they know what they need to do but just cannot get moving. Yes, *follow-through* is almost always *the* hardest part.

Why *don't* we do what we're supposed to do? Especially when it feels so good to do it in the first place? "I'm a procrastinator." "It got lost in the shuffle." "I have a hard time following through." "There aren't enough hours in the day." "I don't have enough energy." "I'm way too busy!" People make these comments to me constantly in therapy, noting them as *major* roadblocks and sources of frustration.

---

21   Romans 7:15.

The truth is, we end up putting more effort into maintaining our cars and houses and even taking care of our pets than we do ourselves. We do everything and anything but attend to our own emotional health. This is a real problem.

We are often thwarted by competing demands, and for most of us, it's not a matter of not knowing what to do but a lack of time and momentum for follow-through. Being wildly busy is often the culprit when it comes down to getting the *emotional tune-up* job done. Ironically, when we are filled with adrenaline and anxiety, this is the exact time we need strong self-care routines to anchor us the most. Investing time in evaluating things like our thinking patterns, recreation time, diet, sleep, and relationship quality can pay off in terms of the stress bottom line.

> **Bottom Line:** By the way, if you're dealing with anxiety, try giving caffeine a break. There's a lot of research indicating that putting a stimulant in your central nervous system when you're overstimulated may not be the best idea. No offense, Dunkin' Donuts, but maybe America should try running on something else?

When we're running in so many directions, it's hard to stop and think of the consequences of self-neglect. I see firsthand what it looks like, and it is very sobering. I work with executives, professionals, pastors, parents, college students, tradespersons, and law enforcement officers who all share the fact that they "never saw it coming." They're on the cusp of burnout, surprised at how their bodies and minds have fallen prey to their own unique professional perils and the pressures of adult life. It often takes a big wake-up call to get us moving toward changing our lifestyles to help prevent stress from getting the best of us.

Caring for oneself

Nothing you are working toward is worth achieving if you are not well enough to enjoy it. It's often said that "you don't have anything if you don't have your health." I would extend this to include *peace of mind* and *emotional and mental health.*

Self-care

We therapists have all kinds of great lingo. "Self-care" is one of my all-time favorites. It's a little generic, no? When people first hear that term, they sometimes think it means spalike pampering or self-indulgence. Others worry that by investing too much in this, they will feel selfish or as though they are neglecting the needs of others. Self-care, however, is a *necessary,* not a selfish, endeavor. It allows us to stay emotionally healthy and resilient and even equips us to encourage others to do the same.

If we're constantly running on fumes, we're often not able to be fully present with the people we care about. Picture yourself on a plane. It's always a bit counterintuitive that we are told, during the flight's safety spiel, that we must put on our own oxygen mask before putting an oxygen mask on a child. But this ensures our ability to help the child. In a similar fashion, self-care strengthens us and, in turn, those we care about.

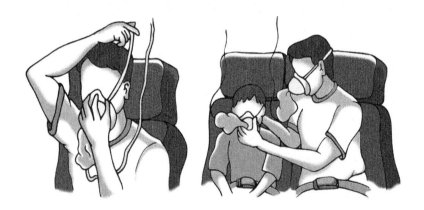

Self-Care Requires Putting Your Mask on First

> **BOTTOM LINE:** There's something to learn from airplane protocol. Putting our masks on first ensures that we stay strong, thus equipping us to fulfill our roles more effectively.

Self-care can be thought of as fine-tuning, emotional maintenance, mental hygiene, a wellness plan, or even getting our butts in gear! What's important to remember is that self-care practices can not only help keep us on track but also keep us moving in the right direction over the long haul.

Most people stop doing things that would, in fact, help them sustain their health and well-being. I could take any of these practices—the way we play, the way we laugh, the way we sleep, eat, touch, and interact—and give you a long-winded explanation about their impact on our well-being. It's not that we lack documentation on any of these topics. Common sense, right? When we laugh and play, we feel happier. When we're well rested, we feel less grumpy. When our tanks are filled with the right food, we feel more regulated (with the exception of Mr. Eats All, of course!). When we're exercising, we have more energy. When our finances are in order, we don't worry so much. Even though this is common sense, we often have trouble following through. Why is it so hard to stick with things that bring us stability and relief?

Most times, we don't stop to consider the long-term impact of neglecting these important aspects of our lives. Over time, we stop noticing just how affected we are by the various strains we experience—whether physical, financial, emotional, environmental or other. Did you know that if you place a frog in warm water and gradually increase the temperature to boiling, it won't detect the changes and abandon its dangerous environment? However, if you were to plop that same frog straight into boiling water, it would instinctively hop out. Like frogs, we become desensitized to the toxic nature of our immediate surroundings. When we are engulfed in polarized political climates and economic crises, along with our unique personal circumstances, it can become difficult to determine that we need to make changes and rely upon specific coping strategies to avoid personal disaster.

Certainly, life's intensity dial can turn up fast, without fair warning. When possible, preventing reaching *that* boiling point is the way to go. Even when something terrible and unexpected happens, if we've minded our self-care, it can help us be more grounded and resourceful in taking a suitable course of action.

Prevention is less costly and more effective than "repair," and it helps us avoid personal and sometimes communitywide catastrophe. It's so much easier to prevent something than to pick up the pieces after the fact. This premise holds true in social work, psychology, leadership, economics, public health, medicine, and education, and it is just plain common sense. You'd rather avoid falling into a hole than climb your way out of one.

Therapy. As with most things, therapy is not like it's shown on TV or like the prevailing stereotypes. I often hear people say, "I shouldn't have waited," after they realize that therapy is much different from what they had thought it would be. But who can blame anyone for being reluctant? Think of the words we use in relation to getting this kind of support. *Psychotherapy.* Am I *psycho* if I need it? *Disorder.* There are scores of "disorders" one may be labeled with. *Mental* health. Am I *mental* if I need help? We've come a long way in overcoming these ways of thinking, but there's still a ways to go.

When we pay attention to the inevitable emotional versions of "rips" and "infections" we experience, we are better equipped to stay healthy. It's when we think "we're all set" and we have "no problems" that we're really in trouble. Prevention is key.

Therapy does a world of good, as it allows us to have support in making meaning of what is happening around us and within ourselves. There is something powerful about being able to talk things over with someone who is trained in human behavior and who will listen and offer objective feedback from a neutral, caring, nonjudgmental standpoint. A therapist's agenda is to help support the needs of each person who walks through his or her door. Therapists help assess what's happening, facilitate the development of a treatment plan that makes sense in light of our life variables, and then help us follow through with it. When we get stuck, a therapist can help us problem solve and look at our circumstances from different angles. Therapy allows for the confidentiality we need to explore difficult emotions and situations without fear that what we say will get around or be held against us in some way.

Fortunately, more than ever, we seek out coaches and therapists for support. The stigma that counseling once carried has been reduced, though not completely eradicated. Globally, we still have a long way to go to ensure that mental health care is accessible. In the United States, the wait times are increasing, and across the world, there are many places where therapy is nonexistent. The World Health Organization describes a projected critical shortage of mental health workers in the next decade.

When services are available, women are more likely to reach out for support—for both themselves and their children. Men, however, need some nudging. Some men struggle in being proactive about their emotional health needs. It's not a failing on their part, just part of ingrained patterns of thinking resulting from stereotypical gender-prescribed beliefs that "real" men have to "tough it out." It's often the case that men have faced a lifetime of conditioning that encourages them to have a stiff upper lip and avoid showing emotion. This creates a perception that getting help somehow signifies weakness. Such pressures immensely hurt not only men but also all of society.

BOTTOM LINE: Therapy and self-care practices are not just reserved for the so-called sick but also help the "well" stay well. Therapy is no longer an excavation of childhood skeletons, but a practical, proven, powerful way to facilitate emotional health by setting and achieving goals.

The statistics are grim. Many men commit suicide on the very day they finally made their first therapy appointment, a sobering reality that affirms their tendency to wait until reaching the breaking point. Fortunately, according to the National Institute of Mental Health, we have come a long way, with men comprising 37 percent of people in therapy. Still, one in five men say that they "don't trust therapists." They should meet us before they decide. We're not that bad, I promise.

Men are certainly not the only ones duped into thinking that therapy is reserved for emergencies only—if then. Most people wait too long before reaching out and getting support. When it comes to preventing anxiety, a lot of us get so freaked out by anxiety that we automatically think something *dreadful* is happening. It takes finesse to figure how to give anxiety enough healthy respect to manage it, while also knowing that it is a very natural response to life's blasts of stress. The success of this kind of approach is demonstrated in countless scientific studies and sound medical evidence.

Fortunately, mental health education is gaining traction, and understanding is increasing about the value of attending to signs of stress before anxiety becomes unmanageable. We're recognizing the critical nature of prevention in helping stave off crises with damaging consequences.

> **Bottom Line:** Anxiety is a big deal to experience but not always a big deal to treat. But the longer you wait, the more complicated it becomes. We're not doing ourselves any favors when we ignore our body's warnings.

Nonpsychological impacts on mental health. Disruptions in mood or happiness can have a lot to do with our body chemistry. There are many medical conditions that have a dramatic and direct link to our mental health. When emotional distress escalates, a wise first step is to check with your primary care physician to see if there may be a medical explanation. It's not uncommon that thyroid problems, low vitamin D, diabetes, or other metabolism-related issues end up being uncovered even before physical symptoms manifest. Early in my training at Boston University, we were told to always "rule out medical issues" before deciding if someone was experiencing clinically significant mental health issues.

This is something my family learned when my niece Kendra experienced a downward spiral in mood and behavior that has given my sister enough material for several books. When Kendra was bounced between psychiatric hospitals and slapped with multiple diagnoses that just didn't seem to tell the full story, I finally said to my sister, "I think something is actually wrong with her brain." What I meant was that her symptoms didn't seem to fit within the purely mental health realm. Soon after, Kendra had a seizure, and it was discovered that she had astrocytoma, a cancer of the brain. After a long and grueling recovery process, including two major surgeries, radiation, and all hands on deck, Kendra has finally overcome many of her challenges and is back to her old self.

In addition to possible medical issues, sleep, diet, and exercise have a major effect on well-being, making a huge contribution toward our emotional health bottom lines. Physical health and emotional health are intertwined, influencing our on our energy thresholds. We can detect a lot by examining our eating, sleeping, and exercise routines. It can become difficult to implement solid routines when our systems are out of alignment. We'll look at the connection between physical and mental well-being more closely in part 2.

> BOTTOM LINE: Wake up! Sleep is powerful! The CDC reports that one out of four US adults don't get enough sleep at least half of the time. Both teens and adults alike report getting less than six hours nightly, instead of the recommended seven to nine hours. Sleep deprivation impacts bodily processes involving hormones, glucose, insulin, pain response, and inflammation. Sleep deprivation also affects mood, motivation, and metabolism. When we're not rested, we're less apt to function at our best.

In addition to considering your physical health status, it's important to reflect upon what "runs in your family." In a routine physical, a family history is always gathered to determine whether diabetes, high cholesterol, heart problems, and so on, have affected people in your family's lineage.

Likewise, mental health practitioners take all of this into account when evaluating a person's emotional state. Gone are the Freudian days when a complex psychoanalysis was used to pinpoint some personal failing as the reason for emotional unrest. Just like other gains in medicine, we have much more sophisticated means of evaluating and intervening when it comes to emotional health issues. I had my ACL (anterior cruciate ligament) repaired in 1992 and again in 2002. Over ten years, the surgery had completely changed. The second time around, the process, recovery time, and scar were far less intrusive than during the prior decade. Continual advances are made in science and medicine over time, and, fortunately, the same is true in mental health.

Family history. Practitioners now understand the importance of "biopsychosocial evaluation." This evaluation of patients or clients incorporates, among other things, health status and important information about what types of emotional disruptions family members have encountered, such as irritability, learning difficulties, trouble with impulse control, mood and memory inconsistencies, or tendencies toward aggressive or addictive behaviors. If family members have wrestled with difficulties at home, work, or within relationships, it's often an indicator that there may be a tendency, or "predisposition," for other family members to experience similar struggles.

I often say that *every* family has evidence of emotional disruption—and most have quite a bit. It's not always in the forefront, since past generations have different notions of such struggles and may be reluctant to share them or do not know what exactly to make of them. For example, Cousin Brian's quirks, Dad's insatiable temper, Aunt Mae's drinking, or Brother Ken's lack of a filter may be easier to make sense of in today's context where information that helps explain behavior is widely accessible and often much discussed.

By exploring family history, people can often find a genetic disposition to certain forms of anxiety and depression in their lineage. Take a moment to consider how your parent(s) and other caregivers(s) managed stress, whether there is a history of substance abuse in your family, or if many siblings or cousins seem to have symptoms of ADD/

ADHD, for example. Chances are that there are some strong tides in your DNA that will be important to consider as you make sense of your own mood cycles, academic/work trajectory, and emotional history.

Term	Definition	CONSIDER THIS
Biopsychosocial assessment	Model that helps build clear, constructive treatment goals based on biological status (medical conditions, family predispositions), psychological forces (e.g., work stressors), and social forces (e.g., difficulty accessing resources).	This type of exploration can help paint a truly well-rounded picture of what's happening, accounting for various dimensions of functioning to help you develop and implement useful goals and strategies.

The larger context

Even when you can't find something medically significant in your history or you don't see a pattern of distinctive issues in your family, anxiety—in one form or another—is still often a reality for most of us. This is because, regardless of personal history, we are all affected by the pressures inherent in the larger society around us. These add to the complexity of our struggles—and of our ability to handle them.

Too often, understandably, we want to rush to make sense of stress that is affecting our lives. Sociologist George Ritzer calls this phenomenon the "McDonaldization of society," where we are in hopes of a "fast-food" solution or formula instead of developing deep understanding of complex issues. Our social science disciplines initially were so focused on internal, individual characteristics and immediate family circumstances that they did not devote enough attention to looking at how society influences our well-being. But none of us lives in a vacuum that protects us from experiencing anxiety. The more we recognize the impact of societal forces on us, the less we will be inclined to inaccurately label or blame ourselves and others.

> **BOTTOM LINE:** We shouldn't rush to judgment when it comes to understanding our mental health. Understanding the complex interchange between biological, physical, social, and environmental factors is extremely important when we interpret emotional functioning and needs.

Freeze, flight, fight

Whether we are male, female, transgender, or nongender conforming, we all face anxiety as human beings. It can surface for a variety of reasons, and it differs for individuals in various situations. Humans' original anxiety reaction has been described as "freeze, flight, or fight"[22] responses, which are mechanisms that can be both incredibly useful and destructive. Freeze, fight, or flight can be a helpful way to understand how anxiety impacts us.

There are two sides to each of these responses to threat or anxiety. Let's start with the useful part. These three *f*'s are part of human design that allows us to respond to a threat. An initial confrontation brings on each response. Freezing is a time to collect momentum and devise a potential plan; flight involves being able to escape when needed; and fight helps us to defend ourselves.

However, when any of the *f*'s escalate, it can work as a disadvantage that leaves us paralyzed, ready to blow up, or ready to run away—not necessarily the best long-term solutions for dealing with what's at hand.

- When we are in *freeze* mode, a temporary paralysis washes over, as though we were deer caught in the headlights. Our bodies are engineered for this type of reaction, giving us time to focus on what's impending. However, if soon we cannot

---

[22] Walter Cannon coined the phrase "fight or flight" back in 1929, and since then researchers have added "freeze" to the list to reflect a more precise scientific description.

move forward—if we remain paralyzed emotionally—we can, like the deer, get run over.

Freezers often stay stuck and have trouble moving beyond those initial stages of fear, leaving them slow to recover and move forward. Over time, some freezers are prone to withdraw, use alcohol or drugs to cope, or "veg out" on video games, TV, Facebook, and the like.

- *Flight* involves detecting danger and causes us to want to get out of a situation that feels unsettling—fast! Fliers typically avoid situations that have the potential to be anxiety provoking, which can end up adding fuel to the fire and interfere with a more rational, thoughtful response.

  Fliers have to deal with the aftermath of hurt feelings, damaged relationships, and other problems created when they leave a situation or relationship because they have become too wound up and anxious. Fliers become agitated and make rash decisions; sometimes they get so excited that they drive everyone around them a bit crazy.

  Other fliers tend to jump from one big idea to the next, taking wild chances and abandoning reason in search of some pie-in-the-sky fantasy. When things get intense, fliers often exit stage left, missing the chance to learn to tolerate and work through uncomfortable moments. One of the most natural but unhelpful responses to anxiety is to try to avoid it altogether. Research has shown that gradual, controlled exposure to stressors in the right proportions can be beneficial; eventually, the trigger becomes benign. But exposing oneself to things that make one anxious takes a measure of resolve to stick around and work through uncomfortable feelings.

- The *fight* part involves becoming argumentative, defensive, and even combative—verbally or physically. Fighters tend to have trouble with confrontation and, automatically, they become reactive. They're on guard, pulling out the figurative sword or boxing gloves in an instant—bam!

Fighters need support in increasing their tolerance for distress and working to stick things out without exploding. Often when people go from zero to sixty miles per hour in their anger, they have a hard time with controlling their emotional outbursts. Anxiety and anger, in these situations, are often more intricately linked than we imagine.

Education about mental health issues is vital

Without a clear picture of the physiological and psychological responses that anxiety produces, it's no wonder that anyone experiencing it would be terribly frightened and unsettled. Education is clearly a vital aspect of preventing and treating mental health disruptions. Fortunately, we're making steady progress in the department of increasing awareness of what "normal" and "expected" reactions to stress can look like.

Recent attention on people who suffer from post-traumatic stress disorder (PTSD) has helped illuminate the need for treatment. Postwar veterans, who have high suicide, PTSD, and depression rates, have brought increased public awareness and access to needed services. PTSD is also highly prevalent among survivors of abuse, accidents, and other traumatic life events. Highly unsettling and disruptive, PTSD warrants specialized support and attention. Hopefully, this type of widespread awareness about those struggling with PTSD will help people with other types of mental health disruptions seek support. By destigmatizing treatment and demonstrating its value, we may become more able to avoid reaching our breaking points and to get the help we need instead of suffering needlessly.

Unfortunately, many people are so afraid of mental health issues that they tend to ignore their red flags entirely. People lump any semblance of struggle into this seemingly dark category, rather than understanding the normalcy of having anxious and depressed moments. As humans, we are bound to experience vulnerability as we try to navigate in a tremendously complicated world.

Medication. Another consequence of our society's general lack of awareness about mental health issues is the tremendous increase in prescriptions for drugs to deal with anxiety and depression. The United States and New Zealand are the only two countries where direct-to-consumer, or DTC, advertising of prescription drugs is legal. In 2012, the pharmaceutical industry made a whopping $83.9 billion! Drug companies know full well that this type of advertising brings home the bacon for them.

Long-term medication. The impact of this is frightening, particularly when children are put on medications at an early age. Side effects and long-term use can be highly detrimental to one's health. I've worked with a lot of adults in their twenties who were put on stimulants in middle school. They didn't receive treatment or education about either executive functioning or the ADD/ADHD spectrum—they were just put on medication and kept on it for years and years.

Many in this situation arrive for therapy with me feeling stigmatized, anxious, and insecure about their abilities. They often want to stay off of their medication but need some practical strategies on how to leverage their strengths and improve their focus, memory, and mood. Like Michael Phelps, whose mother took him off the medications his doctors placed him on, many people who experience ADD/ADHD symptoms benefit from engaging in intensive exercise and activities they love. This, along with supportive therapy, can go a long way.

Weight gain. Weight gain is one of the biggest problems associated with psychotropic drugs. I once challenged a drug rep on this, and he told me, "Well, it's not proven that this medication causes weight gain, but it does increase appetite and cravings significantly." Hello! He thought this was a slick answer, but really, if you crank up someone's hunger, isn't it safe to assume that weight gain will naturally result?

Do we need all these medications? Powerful ads by self-interested drug companies have led many consumers to think that drugs are the best—or even the only—way to respond to stress overload. The problem is, their messages neglect to tell the public that "symptoms" of an "illness" (which may actually just be common, healthy reactions to life's circumstances) may be relieved by a whole host of other remedies, including diet, exercise, sleep, therapy, and improving our environment. Further, other underlying factors—such as low vitamin D, low iron, thyroid problems, or other imbalances—may be the culprits wreaking havoc with our emotional functioning.

Direct-to-consumer ads are crafted in the same fashion through which many products are sold: appealing to our senses and cravings for instant gratification. Some of the depression-medication commercials make it seem as though taking these drugs is a whimsical and even carefree thing to do, like eating candy. In reality, they are likely to produce unpleasant side effects and potentially get in the way of healthier treatment options. Also, it's not at all uncommon for doctors to prescribe more than one drug, leading some people to be on several medications that may have dangerously conflicting side effects. This can not only harm individuals but also misleads us as a society into believing that these drugs will free us from our emotional pain and make us happier. In fact, the opposite can be true; when we jump toward medication too quickly, it prevents us from implementing important lifestyle changes that may well lead to nontoxic, long-term, and genuine relief for our anxiety.

Years ago, psychiatrists were the main arbiters of mental health and the only ones who could prescribe related medicines. Now, primary care physicians (PCPs) are able to hand out mood stabilizers, antianxiety medications, antidepressants, and even antipsychotics. I'm hopeful that most PCPs carefully assess a patient's needs and recommend therapy, healthy behaviors, and other lifestyle changes, but I am concerned that such is not always the case. A medication-only approach worries me since it does not fully address the complexity of our well-being and can end up masking a set of symptoms rather than getting to the bottom of things.

It's not that I am entirely against medication—in the right situation, the right medications can do a world of good. But it's frightening that the type of drug messaging discussed here is something we're constantly bombarded with. It leaves out important pieces of education and awareness about emotional health and self-care that need to be front and center. And because it omits these key things, it leaves the impression that one must solve all his or her problems with drugs. People also need to have a licensed, trustworthy practitioner carefully outline the risks and benefits of medication and help determine whether it is needed or if other forms of intervention could be tried first.

I firmly believe that using medication is a serious decision to be taken only after an in-depth evaluation by an experienced practitioner. Some of my closest colleagues and friends are psychiatrists, trustworthy professionals who have intervened in the most complex situations with great results. I'm fortunate that most of the ones I have worked with have been conservative in their prescribing approaches, carefully considering what is appropriate and how combined treatment (meds + therapy) can leverage a person's well-being over the long haul.

There's an adage we often use in mental health: Lots of people who are on medication shouldn't be, and lots who are not, should be. When the underlying mental health issues are left untended, they can bring a person to a boiling point; medication can help bring the brain and body back into regulation. Still, a great deal of discretion must be exercised. This is the time when the expertise of your doctors and therapists, along with a strong support system, are most needed.

> **BOTTOM LINE:** Medication can be a huge help and recalibration if you fall within the range of a clinically significant depressive and/or anxious episode that cannot be treated otherwise. When our systems reach the point where other interventions are not sufficient, medication may be needed. It's extremely important to have a licensed practitioner help evaluate your situation and develop a multidimensional treatment approach. There are many means to treat depression, anxiety, and stress overload that do not involve medications.

Understanding mental health should start early. Understanding of mental health needs to start early—in homes, schools, churches, and other institutions. The frameworks that social workers, social scientists, and medical and human development practitioners offer within the context of a caring, supportive relationship should be available at large, not just reserved for "severe problems" or moments of high anxiety. Waiting for a crisis to hit is *not the time* to try to learn coping skills.

Look at broader context. In addition to discovering "what runs in your family," consider "what runs in society." Historically, institutions in our society like schools, social, and health care organizations have focused primarily on diagnosing, pathologizing, punishing, and blaming people for their problems rather than preventing those problems and rewarding and leveraging the best in people. This has a tremendous impact on our lives and well-being.

When we consider health and mental health, it's just as important to look outward as it is to look inward. Fortunately, society increasingly recognizes that access to resources has a direct link with our well-being. Wouldn't anxiety and depression be a natural response to the stress of not having basic needs met, such as adequate housing, food, or educational opportunities?

Over the past decades, the US government initiated a program entitled "Healthy People 2020" to promote health equity, defined as the "attainment of the highest level of health for all people."[23] According to research, health disparities adversely affect people who have systematically experienced obstacles to health based on their racial or ethnic group; religion; socioeconomic status; gender; age; mental health; cognitive, sensory, or physical disability; sexual orientation or gender identity; geographic location; or other characteristics historically linked to discrimination or exclusion. Healthy People 2020 distinguishes the determinants of health as including the availability of and access to

- a high-quality education;
- nutritious food;

---

[23]   Healthy People 2010, www.healthypeople.gov.

- decent and safe housing;
- affordable, reliable public transportation;
- culturally sensitive health care providers;
- health insurance; and
- clean water and air.

Term	Definition	Consider This
Health disparities	Particular type of health difference closely linked with social, economic, and/or environmental disadvantage.	Such disparities contribute to high levels of stress in our society, having a negative impact on everyone but particularly on those who have a more difficult time accessing health care due to characteristics linked with discrimination.

Bottom Line: The term "mental illness" is enough to make anyone shudder. It conjures up such powerfully negative connotations. It's no wonder that people are afraid to confront any resemblance of poor mental health. It's important to understand that so-called mental illness symptoms are often part of being human. When these symptoms occur, they should signal us to ramp up our self-care efforts, which start with getting to the bottom of what is happening and what can be done about it.

Deficit thinking. We can see that health is tied to many factors relating to access; there is a direct relationship to health disparities and our emotional well-being. From a mental health perspective, those enduring severe hardship can sometimes be mislabeled as "depressed" without taking into consideration the influence of their circumstances on their functioning and health. Most doctors write prescriptions to treat their patients' symptoms, while providing comprehensive prevention and identifying root causes play second fiddle.

However, it's not necessarily the teachers, human service workers, or even doctors who are at fault. We are all operating within a paradigm that has endured for many generations. Within and beyond the media, there is often a rush to blame individuals for their problems without accounting for the big picture—a tendency called "deficit thinking." Unfortunately, without reevaluating such limited, entrenched ways of viewing people and their so-called issues, we overlook a simple fact: building on people's assets can generate a lot more momentum than blaming people and simply putting Band-Aids on as a temporary fix.

Term	Definition	CONSIDER THIS
Deficit thinking[24]	Emphasizes blaming individuals rather than looking at contextual factors that influence behavior and functioning; fundamentally seeks to focus on what's wrong, broken, and needs to be fixed.	Whether you look to the news or just listen in on conversations, you'll notice what seems to be an overwhelming tendency to zoom in on what's not working rather than what is working or on what can prevent problems.

[24] Lois Weiner is an extraordinary researcher and practitioner who discusses the impact of the deficit model on teachers and students in schools.

Redefining "strong," "smart," and "good"

Fortunately, the positive psychology movement and premise of professional social work that emphasizes strengths and looks at behavior within a context is helping to shift the historical tide that has invested *too* much in framing people as pathological and broken. Until now, too little focus has been given to evaluating institutional policies and practices that are harmful and discriminatory and how they fail to contribute to well-being.

Evidence of this shift is seen in the way practitioners are now asking questions. Take professional social work, for example. This discipline has a huge emphasis on what is known as *person-in-environment* theory. Rather than decontextualizing a person's struggles, clinical social workers are trained to examine the host of environmental factors influencing emotions and behaviors.

Term	Definition	Consider This
Person-in-environment perspective[25]	Framework that recognizes that individuals can be best understood by taking into consideration the environments in which they live and work.	Overlooking such influences can result in faulty assumptions and conclusions that often lead to blaming an individual or particular group.

Strengths-based work

Equally important is the focus on uncovering and building on strengths. This shift from looking at "what's wrong" to "what's right" helps practitioners avoid asking only problem-focused questions. It's equally important to uncover and focus on strengths and to examine what's working well.

---

[25] National Association of Social Workers website: http://www.socialworkers.org

This strengths-based approach is central to professional social work practice, but it can easily be adapted to a variety of disciplines and situations. The key is finding the bright spots to build off of, rather than assuming that someone who is struggling needs someone else to come in and save the day. The work takes on more of a shared, partnership focus, where a person feels empowered to make changes that take into account personal resourcefulness, creativity, and resilience to aid in his or her problem-solving and recovery processes.

Term	Definition	CONSIDER THIS
Strengths-based perspective[26]	Framework that considers a person's self-determination and strengths as integral to the process of healing and improved outcomes.	Stress and anxiety can make us feel as though our strengths and resources are buried—it's important to look for them and use them as building blocks for restored well-being.

The essence of this line of thinking is captured in a metaphor developed by Drs. Sam Goldstein and Robert Brooks to help demonstrate the power and relevance of strengths. Both psychologists trained in the 1960s and '70s era; they were seeking ways to move beyond a focus on deficits and toward strength building. Their metaphor of describing individuals with "islands of competence" to build upon has resonated with many. They assert that once such islands are identified, this experience of success can lead to higher self-esteem and sense of capability in facing upcoming challenges. All of our "islands" differ, and their identification in the early stages of development can prove highly beneficial.

---

[26]   National Association of Social Workers website: http://www.socialworkers. org

Motivational interviewing

Motivational interviewing is a method of sifting through problems and finding hidden-gem strengths by asking questions that relate to our strong points; it is a framework that relies on our being able to envision success. When we're saturated with stress, we often stop thinking about our dreams. Having positive mental images is a powerful tool. While working through my graduate degree, I pictured myself cartwheeling across the stage on graduation day! Of course, when the day came, I did not attempt this in my heels, but this specific image, as zany as it was, played a part in keeping me motivated and enthusiastic about the goals and dreams I yearned to make realities.

The motivational interviewing method incorporates what is known as the "miracle question," which is derived from a solutions-based therapy model that works to help us picture life as more positive and therefore enables us to conceptualize the steps to get there. It helps us to build a scaffolding to work from.

Term	Definition	Consider This
Motivational interviewing[27]	Line of questioning and discussion that is collaborative and person centered; designed to guide one toward increased strength and motivation for change.	Stress and anxiety can demotivate us and prevent us from seeing the promise and possibilities around us.

Life coaches and therapists know the power of visualizing positive images. Jim Carey's story made jaws drop when he told Oprah that while struggling to get his career off the ground, he wrote a $10 million check to himself and tucked it into his pocket. He was actively picturing success in his mind's eye, with the mock check as a symbol

---

[27] If you're motivated to do so, check out more on motivational interviewing here: http://www.motivationalinterview.org.

of his aspirations. Three years later, he received that very amount for his role in the movie *Dumb and Dumber.*

Certainly, this isn't to suggest that this exercise would work for all of us or that "success" has to be so lofty—or that it has to revolve around money, for that matter. The idea is that when we keep powerful, specific dreams in the forefront of our minds, we then are able to devote ourselves fully to an endeavor and avoid spending time immersed in unproductive or negative thinking. Envisioning can be a powerful tool to help us get more satisfaction from relationships, work, and beyond. When we develop a clear mental picture of what we want life to be like, it enables us follow suit with actions that support that picture.

When we create a mental scaffolding, we then have a path to taking clear steps toward the changes we'd like to see in virtually any area of our lives: getting in shape, career goals, family communication, and beyond. Picturing something happening, or "mental rehearsal," is a huge component of creating excitement and momentum toward the dreams we want to realize.

> **Bottom Line:** Start asking yourself and others, "What's working well?" "How can I build off that?" and "What will it look like when I reach my goal(s)?" This minor revision in the way you think and communicate can be quite monumental. When we picture "success" and fill our minds with such images, it can prove energizing and productive. Imagining possibilities can help us think outside of the box when we're feeling stuck and unable to see beyond our current state or circumstances.

Appreciative inquiry

Like the tenets of strengths-based perspective and motivational interviewing, appreciative inquiry (AI) is another useful method of building momentum by looking for the best in people and circumstances. In fact, many organizations draw upon this model to evaluate and improve performance. This method is also a lens through which we can see ourselves and the world. It mirrors a method known as "perspective taking" in therapy circles, which essentially means stopping and taking inventory in a big-picture way rather than getting bogged down with the irritating, small worries of life.

Term	Definition	Consider This
Appreciative inquiry[28]	AI is a search for the best in people, our organizations, and the world around us; helps lead to discovery of what gives "life" by focusing on inquiry centered on an "unconditional positive question."	AI can result in increased perspective and insight, which can lead to greater happiness, gratitude, and satisfaction; it allows for a dynamic process of discovery and imagination that can be quite helpful in solving problems and leveraging potential.

Relying on these frameworks doesn't mean that you always have to look at the glass as "half full."[29] In addition to this mix of looking for the positive, evaluating root causes and triggers can also be extremely helpful. Being able to acknowledge both the positive and negative can lend itself to more effective problem solving or a better outlook.

Multiple dimensions

Psychologist Dr. Carol Dweck does much to debunk traditional ways we tend to frame ourselves (and others) starting from a very early age. She describes two versions of this—"fixed" versus "growth" mind-sets. As their names imply, a fixed mind-set is less flexible and subscribes to the notion that an individual's qualities are set in stone,

---

[28] Here's to appreciating the pioneers of AI, David Cooperrider and Suresh Srivastva, two professors at the Weatherhead School of Management at Case Western Reserve University. http://appreciativeinquiry.case.edu

[29] By the way, in fact, the glass is always completely full when you count not just the water, but the air!

creating angst and urgency to prove oneself.[30] Conversely, a growth mind-set embraces a broader, more human development–oriented bent. The philosophy is that basic abilities can be cultivated, nurtured, and increased over time. This growth mind-set accounts for the fact that while failure is often unavoidable, it can actually create the impetus for persistence.

Dr. Dweck cites various examples of extraordinary individuals who struggled and later went on to great achievements, like William Faulkner, Albert Einstein, and Lucille Ball. Among the many ideas Dweck offers is the encouragement to change our outlook by evaluating our mind-sets and becoming *more flexible in how we perceive ourselves and others.*

Just ask Jonathan Mooney, Ivy League graduate. If he hadn't adopted this growth mind-set, he may have succumbed to the low expectations ascribed by his teachers that he'd end up "flipping burgers." Like far too many students, Jonathan got through school by the skin of his teeth and with some serious emotional scars.[31] How can someone who barely passed school end up graduating with honors from one of America's most prestigious institutions? Perhaps our prior lens of "good student" and the associated prized characteristics (sitting still, linear thinking, fact regurgitation) need to be reformulated. People like Mooney help us to have new, exciting conversations about creativity, divergent thinkers, and learning styles that wouldn't have been possible even ten years ago!

We're starting to recognize that people are multidimensional and can be both exceptionally bright and have exceptional challenges. So, yes, a student can have challenges in their early years but find ways to compensate, persevere, and surpass even the wildest of expectations. And we're learning that the difficulties can actually contribute toward success, not interfere, as has traditionally been understood. Talk about good stress!

---

[30]   Check out www.mindsetonline.org to explore Dr. Dweck's incredible work.

[31]   Mooney's poignant memoir, *The Short Bus*, is on my short list of all-time inspirational favorites. It will change your ideas about "normal" and "ability."

Dr. Abraham Schmitt is another poignant example. His book *Brilliant Idiot* left me with permanent goose bumps. Deemed the "village idiot" because he couldn't tie his shoes, he later went through a personal transformation as he struggled through a "mental fog," searching for meaning. He eventually found that he had a profoundly high IQ, along with dyslexia—which helped explain his extreme abilities and challenges. Dr. Schmitt was a prolific social work practitioner who went on to write books, counsel, and teach thousands of individuals over the course of his career.

People like Mooney and Schmitt help us expand our prior definition of "intelligence," as have models of "multiple intelligence" formulated by Dr. Howard Gardner and others. We now understand that there can be profound giftedness and difficulty present at the same time, offering the understanding of how one can be totally "fine" in one context yet disheveled in another. We are learning about the complex ways we can demonstrate our smarts on a variety of levels—and our struggle in one area is not a stamp of failure across the board, as it once was thought to be.

A framework known as "twice exceptional," or "2E," offers a compelling explanation of this phenomenon. People who are 2E are considered doubly exceptional both because of their *intellectual gifts* and because of their *differences.*

Term	Definition	CONSIDER THIS
Twice exceptional (2E)	People who are exceptional because of their gifts and "differences," with both distinctive strengths and limitations.	This paradoxical framework is a great example of human complexity, helping us to realize how detrimental it can be to try to put ourselves in fixed categories or boxes.

One of the heroes in the 2E arena is Dr. Deirdre V. Lovecky,[32] a premiere champion for gifted children who also have learning differences. She helps make sense of the puzzle that frustrates many children as they try to understand their world. Many end up being misunderstood and deemed "lazy" because of their inconsistent tendencies, which unfortunately are most likely to be chalked up to a matter of personal fault.

Consider the straight-A student whose academic prowess is to be envied yet has a hard time keeping his or her temper in check at home. This student's situation may relate to what is known as "asynchronous development," in which children are well beyond their years intellectually but still at their chronological age emotionally. This dichotomy can lead to a lot of head butting and raised eyebrows. Along with Dr. Lovecky, authors Linda Silverman and Susan Baum offer support in better understanding twice-exceptional children[33] (and adults, for that matter). Their line of thinking is a reminder of how complex we all are, often having extremes in our strengths and challenges. This is very human and needs to be taken into account in the ways we depict ourselves and others.

> **BOTTOM LINE:** We are not one dimensional. There are many layers to uncover in our search to explain the unique intersection of our abilities and difficulties and how they affect our functioning.

---

[32] Dr. Lovecky's book, *Different Minds: Gifted Children with AD/HD, Asperger Syndrome, and Other Learning Deficits*, offers a wealth of understanding for parents, practitioners, and individuals who relate to having these distinctive strengths and challenges.

[33] To learn more, you may want to explore articles and books they've penned, along with looking at the website www.hoagiesgifted.org for further understanding.

Anger, depression, and other symptoms

Contrary to popular thought, anxiety is not just about being worried, nervous, or afraid. Intense underlying anxiety can cause anger; at other times, it is associated with the depression spectrum (both unipolar and bipolar) or other complex emotional and processing issues.

Behavioral clinicians diagnose some people as having an "Axis II personality disorder."[34] One of my first supervisors in the field told me that, after trying to intervene with someone with a personality disorder, you "just know" that they are an Axis-II personality due to their marked abrasiveness, self-centeredness, and difficult personality. Regardless of the root causes, those who tend to blow up alienate others and can get themselves in a lot of hot water. Telltale traits of these personality issues include:

- extremes in feelings and expressions of alternating love or hatred
- seemingly "overinflated" and "extremely fragile" ego; need for constant reassurance and validation
- need for control: "my way or the highway"
- intense idealization of others, often coupled with depersonalization
- poor interpersonal boundaries, including trouble with pacing, seeking "too much too fast" from others
- lack of a "filter," with poor communication skills
- difficulty with self-awareness and perceptions of the impact of behavior on others; lack of empathy
- "intense intensity," often irritable and angry
- irresistible charm—when person is "on" they are really "on" (and when "off," really "off")
- deep desire to connect and be understood, but trouble getting there

---

[34] This diagnosis has carried a lot of stigma over time, but fortunately, new developments are leading to better treatment outcomes and understanding of the complex web of trauma often involved in a person's development associated with such struggle.

Term	Definition	Consider This
Personality disorder	A mental health issue that interferes with a person's ability to perceive and relate to situations and people; leads to social difficulties and limitations at work, school, or home.	The three most common include borderline, narcissistic, and antisocial. Therapy can be beneficial, although it's not uncommon for people who struggle with personality disorders to be inclined to resist therapeutic suggestions or conclusions.

Rick's story

Rick Hebert was the quintessential candidate for "anger management." He's been what his family calls a "hothead" his whole life. "I feel like I'm walking on eggshells" is the mantra of anyone in his close circle. His explosive behavior is brought on by even the smallest change in plans, and although he is quick to snap, he is extremely slow in taking any degree of ownership for his behavior. Ironically, he often faults others for his outbursts, adamantly denying that he may, indeed, need to make changes.

This toxic attitude has cost Rick a lot. He has lost jobs, relationships, and precious time because of his ranting and raving. Underneath his fury, Rick lives in a perpetual state of anxiety and depression. Extremely bright, he is frustrated by boredom at work and an injury that prevents him from being outdoors, which he considers his "one escape." He seems to get his only charge when he finds reasons and people to pour his anger out on, bringing a rush of adrenaline that appears to counteract the state of understimulation his body seems stuck in.

Rick refuses to seek treatment, despite the repeated urging of his family and friends. They are all paying a heavy price for his reluctance. He doesn't "believe in" therapy and honestly thinks his behavior is "fine." People in his life have shut down, becoming guarded and revealing very little of themselves to him because his behavior has greatly diminished their trust. The tension is palpable, wreaking havoc on his four children. They have begun exhibiting behavioral and emotional problems at school, and Rick is quick to blame the flaws of the teachers and counselors while failing to take into account the home environment. He won't admit to himself or to anyone else that his behavior is causing great damage.

The final straw came when Rick was running a routine errand. Perturbed by the actions of another driver, he made a gesture, and his behavior quickly escalated into road rage. Rick got out of his car and assaulted the other driver, not noticing the other driver was only seventeen. With a prior record, this foolish move landed Rick in jail and proved to be the clincher for his wife too. Rick had lots of time on his hands while incarcerated, but he still lacked insight into his behavior and was stuck in his viewpoint that he had been wronged by *everyone* and *everything.*

Rick's circumstances may sound extreme, but most of us know people whose stubbornness makes us beyond frustrated. Underneath it all, they are likely very anxious. If you or someone you know has these types of issues, it is imperative to get help. This is essential not only for the person whose behavior is out of bounds but also for anyone who is in a familial, friendship, work, or partner relationship with that person. Regardless of the underlying causes of the problem, holding people accountable for their behavior is *vital.*

BOTTOM LINE: Personality disorders are rare. Whether you have such disorder or whether you know someone with a personality disorder, living with this problem can be challenging. This is a complex and sometimes controversial categorization, and it warrants assessment and treatment approaches from clinicians experienced in this realm.

Rick's struggles, while rare, are familiar to far too many of us. What adds to the challenge is the level of resistance to suggested changes. This resistance is especially pronounced for someone with a personality disorder but is present in all of us. Whether we are in dire straits or experiencing a milder version of stress, it's not always easy to take a closer look at ourselves and seek constructive feedback on how we are coming across and affecting those around us. But in doing so, we develop important insights that may be critical in building more satisfactory relationships.

When we increase our self-awareness and learn to better understand our thought processes, we are bound to find a great deal of relief. Therapists call this "normalizing," which essentially means helping a person understand that the feelings and thoughts he or she is having are common and often associated with a life stage, task, or conflict that is inherently part of the human experience.

Whether or not you have had the experience of being in therapy, the principles in this chapter give you a glimpse of why it is needed, how it can be useful, and what it can look like. Given the unique trials and joys that life brings, it's helpful to explore how we can leverage strengths and navigate these challenges. Committing ourselves to self-care, self-awareness, and skill development can do a world of good.

Looking at the big picture

Stereotypes and stages

Even though great progress has been made and more people than ever are able to get help, there are still far too many stereotypes and a lack of understanding about emotional health. Terms that are laden with heavy-duty stigma—such as "mental illness" and "disorder"—flood our vocabulary. Exaggerated TV and movie images of "deviation" cause people to fear that they are beyond help—when, really, most people are just in need of some minor adjustments within the complexity of life's stages.

Elisabeth Kubler-Ross brought forth one of the most powerful and memorable conceptualizations of "stages" when she wrote *On Death and Dying* in the 1960s. She introduced the idea that, while grieving, we often experience stages of denial, anger, bargaining, depression, and acceptance. Her model, demonstrating the cyclical nature of our emotions, caught on like wildfire and proved enormously beneficial for anyone enduring grief.

Since her ingenious model premiered, other "stages" models have debuted, offering interesting ways of thinking about the ways in which we move through different circumstances. Some examples include stages of adjusting to teaching (and other professions), cultural changes, empty nest, moving from home, and development from birth to death. Sometimes we make the mistake of thinking that development ends after adolescence; however, our developmental process is lifelong, with many different stages to work through along the way.

Piaget, Kohlberg, and others pioneered interesting ways of thinking about how various life stages are likely to bring out specific challenges and responses. There is something very freeing about understanding that certain emotions are associated with certain stages and that these feelings are completely natural and expected in our development. Lots of times, we think we are doing something wrong, when in fact our responses are almost predictable—and what we might call "developmentally appropriate."

Dr. Ross Greene is a champion for relaying this message as he discusses ways to frame child and adolescent development in a more hopeful, strengths-based manner than is often attached to it. He asserts that the "wasted human potential is tragic," referring to kids who are mislabeled and misunderstood at home and school. His ALSUP model—which stands for Assessment of Lagging Skills and Unresolved Problems—is a framework that has proven successful in helping identify specific areas where students need support at certain junctures in their development. He asserts that sometimes what is being asked of students taxes their threshold of coping; pinpointing skills that will help equip them with higher resistance and more resources can make a world of difference.

The old-school way of blaming kids, teachers, and parents for students' so-called shortcomings fails to offer hope for the many kids who end up being thrown away because of their undesirable behavior.

Dr. Greene offers a wide range of practical strategies through Lives in the Balance,[35] a nonprofit organization he founded promoting his Collaborative Problem Solving approach. Instead of overgeneralizing or lumping kids into negative categories, he helps unpack the reasons why kids struggle, and he offers hopeful interventions that can be applied at home, at school, and beyond during various stages of a child's development.

Sometimes kids just need time to mature and develop certain coping and cognitive skills in order to improve their outlook and behavior. The same is true for adults, as well.

The principles embedded in Dr. Greene's work remind me of Dr. Randy Pausch's last lecture. He was an extraordinary researcher and Carnegie Mellon professor who invented the popular Sim City video games. Having terminal pancreatic cancer was the impetus for his delivery of his "last lecture,"[36] poignantly describing his life experiences and lessons learned. The book that told his story went on to be required reading in many high schools because of its powerful message.

Pausch emphasized the notion of "giving people time," as imparted to him by a mentor. This is a reminder of the need for patience when it comes to moving and developing through life's stages. It may seem as though you or someone you love is stuck, but the hope is that, over time, improvements will be realized.

We all fall on the spectrum

Another development in understanding mental health has been the identification of what is known as a "diagnostic spectrum." Outside the realm of typical adjustments and life stages, a persistent disruption in mental health or everyday functioning can be seen as falling on a continuum, often called a "spectrum," with various ranges

---

[35]   Checking out his website, www.livesinthebalance.org, is a must. You will find yourself grateful that he has shared such a wealth of resources freely. From compelling videos to printable checklists, there's a ton of inspiration.

[36]   Grab a box of tissues and brace yourself to be moved—you can watch his famous grand finale lecture online or read "The Last Lecture." The video went viral, and the book became an instant best seller—for good reason.

of severity. Contrary to earlier in-the-box thinking about mental health diagnoses, the spectrum concept enables us to account for the wide variety of struggles, overlapping symptoms, and complex circumstances people face.

Rather than a black-and-white view of having a precise, permanent "diagnosis" or "disorder," the notion of a spectrum helps us think about where someone may fall on it at a particular point in time, and whether her or his experience can be seen as mild, moderate, or severe. Traits can wax and wane, fluctuating throughout the various stages of life. This spectrum illustrates the degree to which someone may exhibit a cluster of particular characteristics associated with a diagnostic construct.

Term	Definition	Consider This
Diagnostic spectrum	A range of linked conditions presenting in various degrees across individuals; examples include autism, bipolar, and anxiety spectrum.	Gone are the days when we are forced to define someone in one-dimensional terms; the lens of a "spectrum" allows us to see the various shades and layers associated with a person and their ways of thinking/being.

Our ways of viewing people and problems have traditionally been one dimensional, with little room for contradictions or overlap. Now we are shifting to be able to see the various degrees to which someone's most pronounced characteristics can be understood. Spectra also help us to see how these traits can be interpreted as both beautiful and bothersome at the same time. Responding to these paradoxes, the behavioral science/social work community is encouraging everyone to roll up their sleeves, find the good, and build upon it while providing support and skill development in the areas of struggle.

Consider the nuances that can exist within individuals showing up on the following spectra (note: these are generalized and thus not true of every person showing up on such spectra):

- **Autism:** Difficulty with social skills, coupled with fierce loyalty and devotion
- **ADD/ADHD:** Inconsistencies in sustaining attention; can either "tune out" or "hyperfocus in" to be able to solve complex problems
- **Bipolar depression:** Difficulty with mood regularity, often combined with intense energy, personality, passion, and drive

Dr. William Pollock is a gritty Boston doc who likely makes his awestruck residents chew their nails in his presence. He knows his stuff and is highly admired for his brilliance and clinical savvy.[37] A few years back, I heard him speak at an autism conference at Harvard. He approached the podium and exclaimed, "When are we going to realize that *we're all on the autism spectrum?*" This was met with wild applause from over a thousand experts in their respective fields (including social work, psychology, education, medicine). This is because, after studying this phenomenon in depth, many of us can identify within ourselves inconsistencies and quirks associated with autism and other spectra (such as fixed interests, trouble in social situations, sensory overload, etc.). Often, such quirks are exacerbated by certain environmental circumstances and are not just an indicator of "symptoms."

Treatment can help in figuring out if and where someone may fall on a diagnostic spectrum. It can lead to an increase in coping skills and useful insight, helping us navigate our own unique circumstances and make the most of the resources at hand.

CBT

If you or someone you know seems to identify with the characteristics given on a particular spectrum, one of the most universal treatment interventions may bring great clarity and

---

[37] Dr. Pollock's latest book, *Real Boys: Rescuing our Sons from the Myths of Boyhood* is a must-read.

value. Dr. Aaron Beck[38] is known for development of the premiere form of proven treatment—cognitive behavioral therapy (CBT). CBT is a focused intervention that helps guide us to developing healthy responses to "cognitive distortions," which are unwanted, automatic beliefs and expectations about oneself or others.

This modality is popular because it's so practical—and it works. Thousands of studies offer evidence of its effectiveness in reducing anxiety, depression, substance abuse, and more. It's used to treat a variety of issues ranging from eating disorders to life adjustment, obesity, and relationship distress. CBT helps reduce the tendency to create or be disappointed by unhealthy or unrealistic expectations.

Term	Definition	CONSIDER THIS
Cognitive behavioral therapy (CBT)	Treatment intervention used by therapists to support development of skills that help dispel distorted beliefs and modify behaviors.	The way we think impacts the way we feel and behave; examining this closely can prove extremely beneficial.

CBT gets to the heart of the matter through the mind. It helps poke holes in disruptive "automatic negative thoughts"—we can call them "ANTs"—that can ruin any picnic. We'll examine this more closely in the "End Unproductive Thinking" section.

DBT

Kicking it up a notch, Marsha Linehan brought forth a sexier version of CBT, with an added emphasis on specific skill building. Her iteration, known as dialectical behavioral therapy (DBT), reflects a strong reliance on skills to help counteract too-intense emotions.

---

[38] Dr. Beck's classic book, *Feeling Good: The New Mood Therapy*, has helped millions of us improve our moods and keep our thoughts in check.

Term	Definition	Consider This
Dialectics/ dialectical tensions	The tensions between opposite goals and values inherent in relationships.	Life is filled with emotional inconsistencies, in which we may experience a range of emotions that are in direct conflict with one another.

DBT helps address the dialectical tensions inherent in life. Relationships are complicated, and we often seek both connection and independence. One way to think about it is that we often want to be *a part* of relationships/groups but also want to be *apart* from them at the same time. Conflicts arise naturally in relationships—the push and pull of wanting both to preserve our own thoughts and to remain open and flexible to entertain other perspectives, wants, and needs. We want to belong, yet we want to be independent. This is particularly true in the United States and other "individualistic" cultures where self-reliance is next to godliness. Conversely, collectivist cultures embody a group mind-set, where benefit for the greater good is held to be central. These competing values can often create friction and internal disarray as we participate in relationships at work and home.

Individualistic culture	Collectivist culture
Emphasizes importance of individual self-reliance and encourages greater concern with one's own interests.	Emphasizes importance of reliance on the group and a greater concern for the welfare of everyone.
The United States, Great Britain, Australia, and the Netherlands are all examples of cultures that embody this mind-set.	Singapore, Pakistan, Japan, Columbia, and Finland are all examples of cultures that embody this mind-set.

When Linehan first developed her model, it was targeted for individuals experiencing significant dialectical tensions. Originally, the model was used primarily for those experiencing "intense intensity," or extremes in emotions, which needed more specialized intervention. The treatment became linked to a controversial diagnosis known as "borderline personality disorder" because of its effectiveness with people who have this diagnosis.

Today, the value of DBT is being increasingly recognized as important for developing life skills for anyone wanting to improve and grow, even if you are fairly healthy and emotionally regulated. It is also an intervention that can be widely applied to a host of distressing situations (such as substance abuse, eating disorders, and anxiety) and circumstances to promote better adaptation. A few years back, I began adopting DBT principles in my work and in my own life. Over time, I have come to learn that many specific interventions commonly linked to certain symptoms or diagnoses can be helpful with a wide range of general life circumstances and variances.

ADD/ADHD strategies. A prime example of this is seen within the ADD/ADHD literature. The incredible wealth of knowledge, strategies, and skills put forth by such extraordinary practitioners as Kate Kelly, Peggy Ramundo,[39] Edward Hallowell,[40] John Ratey, and Thom Hartmann[41] are some of my all-time favorites. Even if you don't technically register with an ADD/ADHD diagnosis, can't we all use strategies around time management, relationships, paying attention, managing emotions, discipline, and the like? In such an ADD/ADHD world, these strategies are beyond price.

---

[39] One of the most popular self-help books is *You Mean I'm Not Lazy, Crazy or Stupid?* Ramundo and Kelly, therapists with ADD/ADHD, joined forces to write a liberating collection of insights.

[40] Hallowell coauthored several of the *Distraction* ADD/ADHD works with Ratey, along with some incredibly creative and useful books such as *Crazy Busy: Overstretched, Overbooked, and About to Snap; Worry;* and *Shine.*

[41] Hartmann has written scores of fascinating books across a wide range of topics. His "ADD Hunter/Farmer model" is particularly interesting, as is *ADD: A Different Perception,* along with other ADD titles that can be widely applied in our ADD/ADHD world.

Like DBT skills, ADD/ADHD strategies offer a great deal of support in life management, which is often a significant help in reducing stress. It's well worth seeing if the strategies work for you, regardless of whether you identify with a specific diagnosis. Again, we all technically "qualify" for some diagnosis or show up on some spectrum. Wouldn't it be nice if we could throw out some of the language we use to frame these very human nuances and idiosyncrasies?

Term	Definition	Consider This
Dialectical behavioral therapy (DBT)[42]	Form of therapy focusing on emotional regulation, distress tolerance, interpersonal effectiveness, and mindfulness.	These are life skills that apply to daily living. Putting them into practice is beneficial personally and to those around us.

DBT is gaining momentum since it helps bridge the million-mile march between our intellectual and emotional sides. What our head and heart know are often in conflict with one another. When we are first faced with something we perceive as threatening or difficult, we have raw, visceral reactions and let our feelings do the talking—instead of balancing them with what our brain is telling us (remember the bitter lemonade?). On one hand, our heart represents our emotional responses. It allows us to love deeply, feel intense happiness, and experience deep hurt. However, if we were to operate completely out of our heart, we would likely be irrational and impulsive. On the other hand, our brain represents critical functions, such as reasoning and linear thinking. We need it to drive a car, follow a recipe, and solve an equation. Yet if we operated entirely from this domain, we would lack

---

[42] There are some interesting articles at www.dbtselfhelp.com written by people who practice DBT. Remember, you don't need to identify with the characteristics of Borderline PD to be able to put these skills into play to help you adapt and cope.

zest and feeling. The intellectual is certainly necessary, but without infusion of emotions, we would likely be bland and disengaged.

Wise mind and emotional regulation. DBT asserts that meeting in the middle and employing our "wise mind" makes for a healthy blend of being. When we are able to integrate both perspectives into our decision making, communication, and behaviors, it makes a world of difference. The saying "be like Teflon" encourages us to let things to slide right off us. Letting things slide is, in fact, an important life skill. Rather than getting whipped up over all the things coming our way, we can learn to move away from an intensive negative barrage of feelings and instead give ourselves time to address something upsetting from a wiser and less emotionally charged mind.

DBT helps us operate from this "wise mind" vantage point through specific avenues of self-care and emotional support. One fundamental aspect, known as "emotional regulation" (ER), is key to so many facets of our functioning. It's a fancy way of saying that we can learn to keep our emotions in check. ER is central to our well-being, allowing us to monitor our emotional reactions and keep them under control. Emotional regulation can be extremely difficult to achieve under stress or when we are prone to emotional highs and lows. It takes self-reflection and a willingness to receive constructive feedback from others to get a realistic picture of how we're faring.

The ability to use our wise mind also relies heavily on a multidimensional self-care plan that we practice regularly. For some of us, emotional regulation fluctuates because of our natural body chemistry, the amount of sleep we're getting, our diet, and the types of stressors we are facing. It also depends on our reasoning and communication skills and the environment we find ourselves in on any given day. We'll talk about this more in the "RESET Principles" section.

Term	Definition	Consider This
Emotional regulation (ER)	The ability to be aware of one's emotional responses, inhibiting and modifying them to promote adaption and appropriate coping measures in a given situation.	ER is critical in every facet of living; it requires constant reframing and work to keep our emotions in check.

Mindfulness. Mindfulness is another central component of DBT that helps us stay focused. It builds off the wise mind, an optimal way of operating. When you are in a wise-mind state, effectively balancing what your head and heart are telling you, you are best positioned to draw upon mindfulness principles. It may seem simple, but paying attention in very specific ways to what our "gut" instincts are telling us can be beneficial. Mindfulness helps us stay focused and present in the moment—*with* the people we are with and the activities at hand. When we are mindful, we are more apt to act in ways that reflect our intellectual and emotional best.

Term	Definition	Consider This
Mindfulness[43]	A spiritual or psychological faculty that leads to a state of active, open attention to the present where a person is focused upon feeling states and present activities without getting entangled in mental chatter.	Being intentional and deliberate about emotional responses and bodily states can help keep us well-grounded; it's wise to stay tuned to this in order to be mindful of the big picture.

---

[43] www.mindful.org offers some practical strategies to improve mindfulness.

Mindfulness helps us connect our heart and head and avoid the tendency to either overintellectualize our feelings or blow them out of proportion. It encourages us to relax, observe in a neutral way, and not cast harsh judgments on ourselves or others. It helps us avoid living by the emotional seat of our pants, taking the bait on everything unsettling that comes our way. Mindfulness can help us avoid stunting our feelings and becoming emotionally constipated, bankrupt, or disconnected. Mindfulness allows us to be present and participate in the moment at hand, rather than being disrupted by competing emotions or past or future events.

> **Bottom Line:** The skills of emotional regulation, distress tolerance, interpersonal effectiveness, and mindfulness are central to our well-being. The DBT framework offers a great structure for self-care and life skills. It helps us remain tuned in with ourselves and with the people in our lives.

Distress tolerance. Part of regulating emotions involves the ability to deal with the inevitable annoyances and heartaches of life. Some things invariably clobber us and throw us off track. Life's disruptions can range from the minute to the earth shattering. Embracing a mind-set that suffering can help us grow is challenging but necessary. This mind-set is known as "distress tolerance." It can be very difficult to embrace since it's hard to appreciate the benefits of struggle when we're smack in the middle of challenging circumstances.

> **Bottom Line:** Using our "wise mind" is a bit tricky when we're under stress, but with regular practice, we can learn to operate in an emotionally regulated way that helps improve our ability to tolerate distress and roll with the punches.

Paul Tough, author of *How Children Succeed: Grit, Curiosity, and the Hidden Power of Character*, encourages parents and teachers to avoid protecting kids from life's bruises and instead help them work through them. That's what distress tolerance is about. It's about riding the storm and finding resources to help you regroup—in whatever fashion and time frame you need, given all the variables at play.

Term	Definition	CONSIDER THIS
Distress tolerance	Helps us cope and survive in situations where immediate change is not possible or even appropriate.	Being able to tolerate suffering and distress are essential life skills requiring recognition of their importance and regular practice; RESET strategies can help provide a needed safety net in our most trying moments.

Interpersonal effectiveness. Given the extraordinary challenges of life, we need other people to support and help us along the way. Another major aspect of our well-being and skill development includes our ability to work with, get along with, and relate to others. This is another tenet of DBT, known as "interpersonal effectiveness." Our effectiveness in relating and connecting well with others is an important indicator of our emotional health. Sometimes interpersonal effectiveness can be compromised in high-stress moments or when we've had negative experiences with others that reinforce our insecurities, bringing out the worst in us.

Term	Definition	CONSIDER THIS
Interpersonal effectiveness	The ability to develop and maintain relationships through positive communication and interactions.	Healthy relationships contribute to our well-being. Communication and interpersonal skills matter.

We sometimes lose jobs, relationships, and opportunities because we have difficulty communicating and relating effectively. Interpersonal effectiveness relies heavily on our capacity for emotional regulation and distress tolerance. If we are moody or irritable, it becomes very difficult to have positive interactions with those around us. When we are perpetually riled up, operating in an unwise state of mind (either way too much or too little emotion), it can disrupt our ability to participate in relationships in a full and healthy way.

People skills are essential in building happy, healthy relationships with others. Whether at work, school, or home, being able to relate, communicate, and connect goes a long way. This doesn't come naturally for everyone. "Relationship experts"—from Dale Carnegie to Harriet Lerner to Terry Real to Gary Chapman to numerous others—champion the ability to communicate and care for one another. You can see by all the voices out there on these matters that it takes practice and a lot of patience.

This ability to relate to other people has also been framed as "emotional intelligence." This construct emerged from research by psychologists and researchers who began studying the role of so-called people skills, social skills, or soft skills and how they relate to well-being and performance. Daniel Goleman has helped build off earlier researchers Salovey and Mayer to bring this concept to the forefront in the fields of business and psychology. Emotional intelligence is a way of understanding how certain skills and behaviors are helpful in our professional and personal lives. Relationships rely on the ability to read a situation and respond with a certain level of finesse. This seems to be directly connected to adaption and high awareness of self and others.

Term	Definition	Consider This
Emotional intelligence (EI)	Responsiveness, cultural flexibility, empathy, communication skills, humor.	Being "with it," able to think on your feet, go with the flow, put yourself in others' shoes, speak and listen well, and laugh at life's idiosyncrasies (including yourself!).

People with EI are able to maintain better relationships because they "get" how their actions affect other people. They know that how they say something is just as important as what they say. They know that the way they look someone in the eye, the way they listen and respond, can make or break a relationship. When we use our emotional intelligence, we put others at ease; we're able to bring out positive emotions by demonstrating that we "get it" and can respond to their needs and appreciate where they're coming from. Empathy is a telltale feature of EI and is communicated through our words, body language, and even sense of humor.

Cultural flexibility is another key feature of EI. It allows us to appreciate and understand how our cultures impact our perceptions and interactions. Cultural flexibility allows us to see through a wide lens rather than through a narrow, centric perspective.

If we build our social and emotional intelligence, it can be a real asset. When we connect well and are adaptable, it goes a long way. The sooner we can shake things off and realize what's possible and what's not, the better off we often are. Having solid EI skills helps us reflect and be better equipped to engage in healthy relationships.

Nonstop world

Of course, many triggers can raise our stress and interfere with developing our capacity for relationships. Our nonstop world often does not afford us the chance to slow down and think. Many of us are so consumed by the past or the future that it becomes difficult for us to be in the present. On top of that, for many of us, the present is filled with beeping calendar reminders, text messages, e-mails, and the like. Our iPhones and devices are like appendages, making uninterrupted time a rare commodity. The constant distractions blur our focus and undermine our resolve to stay well grounded and avoid complete overstimulation.

It's easy to miss important messages from our mind, body, and spirit. When we operate in a constant fifth-gear, chaotic state, we often lose track of the big picture and get saturated in the details and lose perspective. We get sidetracked; and even if we have time to reflect, it can be challenging to put into practice what we care about the most.

DBT shows great promise in helping when issues have escalated to an unmanageable level. When an individual endures major trauma, combined with other assaults on his or her development, making it through each and every day can be a real challenge. Some aspects of everyday life that many people take for granted are tremendously difficult to accomplish or endure for those wrestling with basic issues of functioning.

ॐ

Dissect and Reflect

As we approach our discussion of the RESET principles, it's a good time to start taking some inventory on how you are faring with self-care and therapeutic practices.

Does this chart look familiar? You saw it earlier in the chapter. Take a moment to consider your responses to the following. Soon, you will have the chance to set some goals around each of these areas to promote your well-being on a variety of levels.

Ingredient	Ask yourself	If not, what's getting in the way?	What is one thing you will start doing now to improve this aspect of your life?
Pleasure	Do I laugh a lot? Have I stopped doing things I once felt were enjoyable? Do I take myself too seriously?		
Sleep	What is my sleep pattern? How much do I get on average? Do I feel rested?		
Exercise	Do I move? Am I regularly working up a sweat? Do I feel healthy and in shape?		
Intake	What am I putting into my body? Is there too much or too little of something in my diet? Am I hydrated? How much caffeine and alcohol do I consume?		

Connections	Do I have a support system? If I'm struggling, who do I turn to? Do I participate in activities outside of work or immediate family? Do my associates lift me up?		
Setting boundaries	Are most of my relationships mutual, or do I tend to be the one giving most of the time? Do I feel stretched by pressures to do for everyone else? Do I feel guilty or have trouble saying no?		
Faith	Do I live true to my convictions and beliefs? Do I spend time nurturing and growing my spiritual side? Am I living for a purpose beyond myself?		

Chapter 3 in a Nutshell
Therapy 101

1. **What works?**
   - Be strategic. Practical plans help us manage life's demands.
   - Meg left self-care on the back burner and lost hair as a result.
   - Jamie's self-neglect was a recipe for disaster.
   - Protective factors help mitigate the vulnerabilities and consequences associated with many forms of stress.

2. **Staying the course**
   - Pleasure, sleep, diet, alcohol, and caffeine consumption impact our potential for coping.
   - Follow-through is often incredibly difficult but worth attending to.
   - It's easier to prevent stress overload than it is to treat it.

3. **Caring for oneself**
   - Having peace of mind and solid emotional and mental health makes what we're working toward more enjoyable.
   - Self-care is a necessary endeavor.
   - Like airplane protocol, sometimes we have to put our mask on before we help others.
   - Prevention is less costly and more effective than repair.
   - Therapy can be helpful in issues ranging from mild to severe.
   - Pay attention to sleep, family history, environment, and context to understand and care for yourself.

4. **Freeze, flight, fight**
   - Freezers, fliers, and fighters demonstrate natural responses to environmental forces.

- Taking medication is a serious decision that should be carefully thought out.
- Mental health awareness should be cultivated early and extend beyond the medication conversation.
- Health disparities are pervasive and need to be addressed to ensure improved collective mental health.
- Deficit thinking is damaging and leads to mislabeling, inaccurate judgments, and missed opportunities.
- Institutions play a major role in shaping our perceptions and have traditionally focused too heavily on blaming or labeling. Social oppression and deficit thinking hurt everyone.

5. **Redefining "strong," "smart," and "good"**
   - Positive psychology and professional social work principles help us to contextualize people's potential.
   - Motivational interviewing and appreciative inquiry are models that flip deficit thinking.
   - Appreciative inquiry helps build momentum by looking for the best in people and circumstances.
   - Dr. Carol Dweck sheds light on ways to adopt healthy views that give us the impetus for improvement and resilience.
   - Jonathan Mooney, Abram Schmitt, and Deirdre Lovecky help reconstruct the notions of "normal" and "exceptionality."

6. **Anger, depression, and other symptoms**
   - Anxiety is not just about being worried, nervous, or afraid.
   - Extremes in mood and behavior warrant attention, since they may indicate a deeper level of distress.
   - Assessment and intervention can help normalize our experience and raise our self-awareness.

7. **Looking at the big picture**
    - Experiencing different stages of emotions are inevitable through life's changes and losses.
    - Spectra help us see the multidimensional nature of people.
    - CBT/DBT emphasizes skill development.
    - Treatment-based principles, such as mindfulness, interpersonal effectiveness, emotional regulation, and distress tolerance offer helpful life skills for all of us, even if we think we are doing "well."
    - Emotional intelligence and staying tuned in to ourselves and others help us identify areas for growth and keep us well grounded.

4

SPRINTERS, SKIPPERS, TUMBLERS

Don't think too much. You'll create a problem
that wasn't there in the first place.
—Unknown

> ESSENTIAL QUESTION: What leads you into
> a downward thinking spiral—or prevents you
> from entering one?

Why me?

The orange dashlight flashed wildly, and the unmistakable sound
of deflation soon followed. Danielle Hopkins's flat tire was just
another mishap in a week that seemed to be fraught with mini-
catastrophes. "Why do bad things *always* happen to *me?*" she lamented.
She rattled off a list of things to support her theory that she was the
only one who ever had such a run of bad luck.

The "why me?" struggle is one of many automatic negative
thoughts (ANTs) that abruptly creep into our brains, especially when

something has just gone wrong. When we stew in negative thoughts, our insecurities mount. In this type of mind space, we become overwhelmed and frantic and lose sight of the big picture.

As we learned in chapter 3, thoughts laced with negativity are known as "cognitive distortions" and are part of being human. Actually, it would be quite bizarre to react to something negative with an automatically sunny response. If someone kicked you, you wouldn't smile. When life hands us something difficult, it takes time to digest and process what is at hand and put it into perspective.

But stress mounts when negative thinking patterns go unchallenged. It's easy to fall into the "why me?" trap, believing that we are the only ones who experience annoyances and heartache. In fact, even people who seem "put together" are managing their own set of worries behind the scenes.

Taking the time to evaluate our tendencies toward negativity can help improve our outlook and greatly control the habit of getting caught in a "stinking thinking" web can that easily entrap us.

In this chapter, let's look at three versions of "stinking thinkers": sprinters, skippers, and tumblers. As you read, think about your own reactions and thought processes in various situations that you face. By taking the time to assess your tendencies in these broad categories, you'll be ready to understand and apply the RESET principles in part 2.

Sprinters rush

Sprinters rush to extremes in judgment. They struggle with personal insecurities and extreme, incessant fears about what others think about their appearance, education, communication skills, social status, or other traits. Sprinters worry about what rejections lie ahead, waiting for "the other shoe to drop," and they continually feel that "something will go wrong." Like leaping frogs, they jump ahead of themselves, automatically assuming the worst. They engage in negative *predictive thinking*, expecting "this is going to be bad," which leads to lots of *anticipatory anxiety.*

Anticipatory anxiety remains a silent killer of social satisfaction and connection. Dr. Srini Pillay,[44] a top-notch physician trained at Harvard Medical School, discusses what he calls "the contentious relationship we have with anticipation," asserting that we spend way too much time embroiled in negative mental gymnastics before an event even unfolds. Dr. Pillay says that we are haunted by questions of anticipation that end up leaving us in a state of fear and unrest. This type of thinking becomes a destructive pattern over time, doing a number on our confidence levels and our enjoyment of life.

Term	Definition	Consider This
Anticipatory anxiety	Concern over future events that typically have triggered worry in the past.	Staying stuck in this mode can waste precious time and interfere with enjoying life and solving problems. Generally, problems are far less insoluble than we imagine them to be.

If you are a sprinter, your anticipatory anxiety causes your imagination to run wild as you entertain thoughts of all of the things that could go wrong in a situation you are gearing up for. Sprinters tend to mentally rehearse conversations and events, but instead of picturing things going well, they worry about *anything* and *everything* that could possibly go wrong.

If you are a sprinter, it is important to consider what your triggers are. The most common include:

- **Being uncomfortable in social situations:** "I won't know/like/connect with anyone," "I feel awkward/less than," "This will be boring/stressful/annoying."
- **Facing a grueling task like a public presentation or demanding meeting:** "What if I mess up?" "This is scary," "I'm not good at this," "What will people think about me?"

---

[44] For more, get your hands on Dr. Pillay's book: *Life Unlocked: 7 Revolutionary Lessons to Overcome Fear.*

- **Attending holiday gatherings:** "Everything has to be perfect," "S/He's going to say something to annoy me," "I feel misunderstood."
- **Confronting serious matters in a relationship:** "I'm afraid s/he will take it the wrong way," "What if they leave me?" "I don't want her/him to blow up."
- **Visiting the doctor's office:** "What if something is drastically wrong with me?" "I'm afraid of how I feel when I get a shot/ am weighed/am asked too many intrusive questions," "I hate long waits."

Certainly, any of these situations can bring us discomfort, but sprinters worry in full force that they absolutely will. This mindset starts to erode any chance of happiness. Sure, holidays, parties, relationship-defining talks, and visits to the doctor aren't always a picnic, but the level of sprinters' intense anxiety is symptomatic of anticipatory anxiety. Their imaginations run wild, bringing on even more uncomfortable feelings of turmoil and unrest.

Remember that *insecurity* is often at the root of the tendency to sprint toward anticipatory anxiety and imagining negative outcomes. It's important to not only practice positive visualization of upcoming events but also to address the underlying insecurities that can unravel us rather quickly.

DISSECT AND REFLECT

- What are some of my triggers?
- How disruptive have they become?
- What tends to help me when I am in sprinting mode?

Rate your expectations of events from 1 to 10 (10 = over-the-top horrible). Do this before you head into a situation that you expect will be taxing. Afterward, rate how the experience actually panned out.

- Did I notice anything different from what I'd expected?

- If it was just as difficult as I'd expected, would I be willing to try it again?
- If so, what do I think would help make it better?

Skippers filter

Like sprinters, skippers experience a great deal of distress as their thoughts unfold. Skippers are experts in filtering out the "good" and zooming right in on the "bad." They pay little attention to what is going well and a lot to what is not. Skippers engage in *mental filtering* and subscribe to the notion that "one bad apple spoils the whole barrel."

Term	Definition	Consider This
Mental filtering	Process of focusing too intently on negative aspects of self, others, and situations.	When we're stressed, it takes a lot of effort to focus on what's working well. Looking for the good can improve our well-being and have a positive impact on those around us too.

Skippers tend to magnify their perceived weaknesses and trying circumstances to a high degree. This way of thinking often manifests early in their lives, whether at home, at school, or elsewhere. Skippers take things personally and often attribute difficulties as a failing on their part. They feel as though there is some element of "deserving" when bad things happen to them. They disqualify anything positive about themselves and the resources they have and instead concentrate heavily on what's not working well.

Skippers carry their proclivity toward filtering into their relationships. Because they view themselves in such a negative light, this spills over into their general way of thinking, and they start also believing that others are out to get them or that they are receiving unfair treatment. They sometimes keep a running chronicle of all the "bad stuff," constantly referencing that long laundry list of *things-gone-wrong* over long stretches of time.

If you are a skipper, it is important to consider if there is a way you can reframe your thinking to help you keep perspective with regard to yourself and others. Some strategies for how to do this are illustrated in the following examples:

- Sam Porter was annoyed by his oldest brother, John, the firstborn in his family, who was constantly bossy. For a long time, this put a major rift in their relationship. Over time, Sam started to notice that while John's take-charge attitude sometimes left everyone annoyed, he was also a leader who made things happen. His assertiveness was not always easy to deal with, but his intentions were good. Even though John was undoubtedly intense, Sam started to focus on the positive, making for less tension and a more enjoyable relationship.

- Mya Brinks loves running and summer. When she broke her ankle only halfway through June, she was stunned. She started thinking about how unlucky she was, lamenting for a few days, until a turning point when her thinking started to shift. While disappointed that she would have to revamp her usual plans, she thought of her cousin Bryan who sustained a life-changing injury that left him needing a wheelchair. His courage and positive outlook helped her refocus on the big picture rather than on her temporary limitations.

- Despite intense nerves, Peng Win managed to complete a presentation at work and received lots of praise from his boss. Even so, he struggled because of some mispronunciations and jitters that he was sure were clearly apparent to everyone in the boardroom. After some time, Peng realized that he had learned a lot through the experience and that he would keep improving with practice. He also remembered how far he had come in being able to stand in front of an audience and deliver a message. Peng was even able to laugh about the nuances of the presentation, which helped defuse his initial tendency to self-sabotage.

DISSECT AND REFLECT

- Do I find it hard to identify the positives in myself, people, and situations? What qualities do I see in myself that are really distinct?
- In what ways do they serve me well?
- What do I need to modify?

As a next step, look for any positives in a given situation or relationship. If you are in the middle of turmoil, it can often prove helpful to wait a little while after you've encountered a challenging situation, when you're in a better frame of mind to try to find the positives.

- If a person is difficult, can I think of some of their traits that I really like or admire?
- If a situation is upsetting, is there a silver lining to be found?
- Is there anything remotely funny about this? (Humor can be a great way to defuse a situation or problem. If you can laugh at yourself or the nature of what you are dealing with, it can bring a great deal of relief.)
- Can I reframe something that I am wrestling with and see it as an opportunity for growth rather than something that constantly disrupts happiness?

Skipping over positive attributes can leave us stuck and discouraged. This can lead to another unhelpful thinking pattern—in which we *tumble* into a great deal of turmoil.

Tumblers spin

Tumblers quickly spin out of control. When something goes wrong, tumblers easily get caught in a cycle of *catastrophizing*. It is as though they have triggered a mental avalanche that sends them toppling over into a deep sense of impending doom and hopelessness. Once this cycle is set into motion, it's hard to regain stability.

Term	Definition	CONSIDER THIS
Catastrophizing	A way of thinking that leads to the belief that the absolute worst is inevitable.	When our thoughts tumble out of control, it can take a toll on our emotions and relationships.

Tanya's story

Ever since her breakup with Syd, her longtime boyfriend, Tanya Kip had a lot of trouble adjusting to life without him. When she started dating again, she was filled with anxiety and ended up clinging too quickly to her new dates, which inevitably led them to shy away from her. After a few sour experiences, Tanya's anxiety was at a peak level.

Triggered by her most recent dating folly, Tanya began catastrophizing that she would *never* be happy again. She started to imagine what life would be like if she were *completely alone forever*. She had vivid images of herself in various situations—dateless at weddings, slumped over alone watching TV, and perpetually stumbling over her words when someone showed up on her attractiveness radar.

Tanya started to internalize the beliefs that she was hopeless, undesirable, and awkward. The problem with this was that her behavior reflected her catastrophic thinking. It caused her to clam up and act conspicuous in social situations. She was so uptight that this "doom and gloom" vibe affected others. Her needy, "try too hard" displays were a deterrent to socializing. It wasn't until she had an honest conversation with her best friend that she was able to see that the worst was not inevitable and that she had to stop letting her imagination run wild. If she continued thinking this way, it would only bring on more heartache, and her aloneness would become a self-fulfilling prophecy.

Tumblers get caught up in worrying about failure. Whether concerning their career, financial, academic, or relational situation, tumblers have an enormous amount of difficulty keeping their catastrophizing thoughts in check when something goes wrong.

For tumblers, it is important to practice "thought stoppage" to interrupt the process of creating negative mental scenarios. Catastrophic thinking causes us to believe that if X happens, then Y will come true. This type of thinking leads us down all kinds of rabbit holes that can be rather damaging. Thought stoppage is a way we can tell ourselves to "knock it off" and stop feeding ourselves such wild stories.

Catastrophic thinking isn't limited to long-term worries; it can be triggered by intrusive thoughts brought on by temporary uncertainty. I remember having such thoughts as a child when my parents were running late, my mind automatically telling me that they had been killed in a car crash. When unfiltered, our immediate thoughts can often be scary and misguided. It's important that we slow down and realize that we are just tumbling into unwarranted anxiety, and we simply need to regroup.

DISSECT AND REFLECT

- What sets my downward spiral into motion?
- Do I notice that my tendency to catastrophize is worse at certain times?
- What, if anything, interrupts these thoughts before I hit a place of despair?
- What helps me avoid or reduce this type of tumbling?

Thought stoppage can be hard to put into place. Our thoughts are very powerful. One way of accomplishing this is to identify your most pronounced fears and insecurities. They are often intricately linked to fears of underperformance, failure, aloneness, or abandonment. Consider whether any of these thoughts sound familiar:

- If I mess up now, I'll never recover.

- If I fail this test, I'll never get into this college.
- If she/he breaks up with me, I'll never find love again.

Next, think about times when you have felt these kinds of thoughts and the outcome was far less terrible that you had envisioned. When something triggers us, we often think that we may never move forward, but we later recognize that the negative experience helped us to grow or even find better circumstances. This is common when it comes to relationships. The person we once thought we couldn't live without ends up being the one we're glad to have moved on from.

Flipping worry upside down

Sprinters, skippers, and tumblers share some common links. In addition to high levels of self-scrutiny, worry, and insecurity, they all reflect positive traits, as well. Our thoughts reflect that *we care*; and, in each instance, our concern that things may go wrong is natural. Often, we are overwhelmed or ridden with anxiety or discouragement; we're not operating at our best—and then we launch the cognitive distortions that twist and spin things into an even more negative light. Because we don't consciously do this, it takes self-reflection and hard work to identify and overcome these tendencies in a way that allows us to have authentic reactions to life's problems without getting to the point that we can't see our capacity to cope and restore equilibrium.

Of course, there is another side to all this. Sometimes people engage in magical thinking or are so laid back that they believe everything will just somehow work out without putting an ounce of planning or effort in. We'll tackle that next.

℘

Dissect and Reflect

- What situations tend to provoke the sprinter, skipper, or tumbler in me?

- Do I have any ANTs (automatic negative thoughts) that tend to reoccur?
- What insecure thoughts are most difficult for me to stop?
- Is there a trusted person in my life who can help me direct my mental process *away* from unhelpful thinking?

Chapter 4 in a Nutshell
Sprinters, Skippers, Tumblers

1. **Why me?**
   - Automatic negative thoughts (ANTs) creep in when we are faced with stress.
   - Marinating in negative thoughts increases our vulnerability and insecurity.
   - Cognitive distortions, a.k.a. "stinking thinking," can entrap us in very specific ways.

2. **Sprinters rush**
   - Insecurities lead us to extremes in judgment.
   - Sprinters assume the worst about themselves and upcoming situations, engaging in "predictive thinking."
   - Anticipatory anxiety leads us to worry over future events that have triggered us in the past, causing our imaginations to run wild.
   - Social situations, public speaking, holidays, confrontations, and even doctor appointments can set off our tendency to sprint.

3. **Skippers filter**
   - Skippers pay less attention to what's going well and more on what's not.
   - Mental filtering leads us to subscribe to the idea that "one bad apple spoils the barrel."
   - Reframing can help us to take things less personally.

4. **Tumblers spin**
   - Catastrophic thinking sets off mental avalanches that trick us into believing the absolute worst is inevitable.
   - When we picture ourselves in dire straits, we can give off a "gloom and doom vibe."

- Thought stoppage can help prevent us from getting too carried away with our wildest worries.

5. **Flipping worry upside down**
   - While deep, intensive thinking can become problematic, it also reflects a high level of caring and concern.
   - Self-reflection can help us reframe our thinking and restore our potential for coping and personal growth.
   - Without any worrying, we may become too lax. This may cause us to avoid initiating activity that can build character and lead to opportunities.

5

There's No Golden Ticket

Oh, you should never, never doubt what nobody is sure about.
—Willy Wonka

> ESSENTIAL QUESTION: How does your version
> of a golden ticket influence how you think and
> what you do?

Waiting for the elusive big break

Who can forget the image in *Charley and the Chocolate Factory* of Grandpa Joe Bucket, housebound, clad in pajamas, being waited on hand and foot until the moment his grandson, Charley, bursts through the door with the coveted golden ticket? Grandpa Joe's triumphant dance is short lived when he finds himself entrapped in the infamous Willy Wonka Chocolate Factory—where the unexpected is expected.

We salivate over the potential of landing our own version of a golden ticket. The right job. The right person. The right paycheck. Something to lift us out of our despair. We strive to be cool, wanted, esteemed, and financially secure. We hold the belief that if *this* happens, *then* life will improve dramatically.

Our thought process goes like this: *If only happens, then I will feel/ be.* Our expectation is that when *that thing* happens, it will suddenly and unequivocally shake things into perfect bliss. There are so many versions of this:

Magical thinking	More likely ...
Once I finish my degree, I will feel ultrasuccessful.	The more you learn, the more you realize how much more there is to understand. You may end up wanting more degrees and credentials even after accomplishing the goals you once may have thought were unattainable.
After I complete this project, things will be less chaotic.	There's usually another project looming ahead and more work to be done. It's hard to have work constantly hanging over our heads, but that's the reality of life.
If only I had this promotion or job, I would be truly satisfied.	Organizational life is complicated, and the dynamics are often difficult across many different fields and environments. In today's market, job security is often shaky. Sometimes the higher you climb up the ladder, the lonelier and more difficult it becomes.
If my brother-in-law wasn't so annoying, I'd be happier.	In-law dynamics are indeed complex! Often, however, the frustrating people in our lives can actually build character. By focusing too much on flaws, we become reactive and unhappy (and maybe not very fun to be around).

If only I were thinner/ richer/more popular/more articulate, I'd like myself better.	Even when we earn more, find more friends, or lose weight, we are rarely satisfied. We find other things to covet, feel bad about, or zoom in on that cause us to form a new "wish list."

When the if-only thoughts flood our minds, it's hard to notice the limitation to this line of thinking because we are under the spell of imagining the "good life" we've constructed in our minds. As you learned from Jim Carey's $10 million check story in chapter 3, the power of visualizing is profound. What's important is carefully selecting what matters so that we're not chasing after something that may not prove as wonderful as we imagine.

When it comes to those elusive golden tickets, many of us have learned that the things we wish and work hard for end up leaving us disappointed. In fact, studies have shown that people stay at a relatively consistent level of happiness *regardless* of whether something exhilarating happens, like winning the lottery, or whether they experience something atrocious, like watching a loved one die. In either case, people eventually go back to about the same level of happiness they felt prior to such a life-changing event. This tendency is known as the "hedonic treadmill"—which certainly pokes some holes in our thinking about golden tickets and such.

Term	Definition	Consider This
Hedonic treadmill	Tendency to return to relatively stable level of happiness despite changes in fortune or achievement of goals.	This overturns lots of conventional thinking about ways to find happiness. Life's most precious gifts are often found in what we already have, not in golden tickets.

Still, we hold on to magical, wishful thinking, hoping that "something big" will happen to bring us to a state of bliss. A fabulous vacation. A warm, fuzzy holiday gathering. A manic concert event. Winning the big sports title. Our real-life moments often pale in comparison to the quintessential glitzy "Hallmark moments" that conjure up images of holidays, vacations, and entertainment experiences as sheer joy. Inevitably, our highs quickly wear off. Vacations can be spoiled by sickness or other calamity.[45] The image of the Hallmark holiday can lead us to believe that happiness *must* happen at a certain time or place or in a certain way. Often, however, because we feel pressure to have a perfect, happy time, the holiday ends up being too chaotic to enjoy—or we end up feeling too burdened to enjoy it. Usually things that are too hyped up are not worth the hype. Yet the power of advertising leads us to believe otherwise. Our expectations are so high around such things that we can easily become disappointed and experience major letdown.

"More" doesn't equal "happy"

In our society, having lots of stuff and money is associated with feeling powerful, content, and "with it," yet it does not give us what we really yearn for: self-acceptance, people that "get" us, and feeling capable of carrying out our purpose and enjoying the many genuine riches we have.

We spend billions on image building—plastic surgery, clothes, cars, and acquiring more and more "stuff" to bolster our self-confidence. Media messages are carefully constructed to undermine that confidence. Companies spend—in order to make—a lot of money convincing us that if we have such-and-such product for our hair, face, floors, or cars, then our level of awesome will skyrocket. We are led to believe that we'll be envied for our sparkle, and people will flock to us if we follow these costly paths to cool.

---

[45] Just ask anyone who has survived one of those petri-dish cruise calamities—yuck!

Some of us are satisfied without a lot of material things but still fall into the "it's never enough" trap in other ways. My vice is reaching goals. I want to be a star in everything I do—at home, work, and beyond. I'm supercompetitive with myself. I strive to get to that next level—only to find that once I'm there, I want more. This is partly due to my zest for life and my intense love for my family and my work. I also love the thrill of planning and am addicted to the adrenaline that comes with accomplishing ridiculous amounts of work. This has served me well in many ways, but I'm maturing and trying to intentionally change my mind-set. I've learned to make a point of slowing down and appreciating what "is" and not always looking for "what's ahead."

If we wait for that makeover, accomplishment, or "next big thing" to make us feel fascinating or legit, we are chasing our tails. Wanting that golden ticket is very human, but carefully evaluating the messages we get from media, our own heads, and others will help us curb our endless pursuit for "something more."

> **Bottom Line:** Wanting what we have and making the best of it can bring contentment. When we chase after a certain image or the golden ticket, we most often find ourselves disappointed. When we reach our goals, it's important to enjoy the moment before we're on to the next big hurrah.

What if?

Another variation of dreaming about finding the coveted golden ticket comes in the form of wishing we could change things that have already occurred: *If only I had done _____, then _____ would never have happened!* This is known as "counterfactual thinking." It's a highly unproductive thought process that leads to rumination and mental anguish.

Term	Definition	Consider This
Counterfactual thinking	Process of imagining alternate versions of reality, based on wishing we or others had acted or performed differently for a better outcome.	When we spend too much time dreaming about "what might have been," we lose sight of "what is" and "what else is possible."

Life's decisions do not always turn out well. Often our decision making is complex, with many things lying beyond our control. Many of us have a tendency to replay conversations and events over and over in our heads, regretting how we handled various situations. Regret is a powerful force, something that most of us wrestle with at one point or another. It leads to thinking narrowly—only about what we could have done differently. In these moments, we often have a difficult time accounting for *other* factors that influenced the circumstances or interaction. Our tendency to get caught in the net of counterfactual thinking makes it tricky for us to see beyond ourselves and realize the importance of drawing rational conclusions.

We can usually brush off having said something foolish or making an embarrassing mistake if it doesn't have huge consequences. It becomes more complicated when we think, *If only I had done something different* to reach an important goal or to prevent a dire situation. In such cases, it's important to take a closer look and evaluate the entire picture.

For example, consider:

- **Time and place:** The era in which we grew up, family we are born into, circumstances that were present and influential.
- **Available resources:** Where we live, work, and study; financial circumstances; support networks; amount of time we have.
- **Maturity/developmental stage:** Our readiness to take on a certain task or solve problems, combined with the available opportunities present that allow us to learn and grow.

- **Personal traits:** Unique temperament, threshold for coping, disposition, learning style, level of intensity, intellectual depth, health variables.
- **Accidents and loss:** Life is fragile. We often think that bad things won't happen to us, but a split second can change everything. No matter how careful we are, bad things can and do happen.
- **Outside influences:** Other people, economy, destiny, chance, God's big plan, and so on.

Lots of times, we forget that all of these factors fall outside of our control. Forgetting this can lead us to constantly second-guess ourselves. The resulting what-if thoughts, arising in different ways for each of us, can be torturous.

Jeanne's regrets

Jeanne Erickson was a whiz in high school but, like many in her day, had little support from her family to pursue college. For years, she struggled with guilt. She loved her family, but she also wanted to have a meaningful career. She spent endless hours frustrated that she hadn't had the chance to go to college and felt low self-esteem for what she perceived as a lack of accomplishment. Jeanne constantly blamed herself and stewed in a sea of negative feelings because she felt so "underaccomplished." Steeped in regret, she kicked herself on a daily basis over this. Jeanne rates high in the "counterfactual thinking" category.

Ronaldo's regrets

Ronaldo Joyce left for work at his usual time. He shortly received a phone call from his frantic wife, after his toddler son took a terrible fall. He instantly thought that if he had only changed something in his routine that morning, maybe he could have prevented the fall. He wished he had taken more time to eat breakfast, shower, or play with his son. He was angry at himself for being so career driven, feeling that he had lost track of what was important. Although Ronaldo was both an accomplished businessman and excellent father, this thought process went on for months. Despite repeated reassurance from others that he had no control over what had happened, it was hard for Ronaldo to see that accidents often fall outside the scope of our control.

Counterfactual thinking is a slippery slope. When something upsetting happens, we instantly want to make sense of it. It's sobering to realize just how little control we have in many circumstances. We are conditioned to think that certain actions lead to certain results. Life tells us something different, which is often very unsettling. Still, we think:

- If X had or Y hadn't happened, my life would have been totally different.
- If I had only done Y, I could have prevented this tragedy.

It's not uncommon to automatically think this way, and it takes time to balance this magical thinking with additional perspective to help counteract the intense, raw feelings we have in the face of distress. This is true whether we are dealing with something considered minor or something that is life shattering.

> **Bottom Line:** There is a great deal of life that falls outside of our control. While we need to step up to our challenges, it is also important to understand what things we must accept and then play the hand we've been dealt.

The myth of balance

Sometimes stress can arise because of our expectations around being "balanced." There are scores of articles, books, blogs, and therapy sessions devoted to "finding balance." It's sure to come up in virtually any stress-busting conversation. People, especially we therapists, are obsessed with promoting this notion of balance, yet in many ways, it is quite elusive.

There's simply too much hype about balance. Life is not balanced, yet we're all chomping at the bit trying to find ways to feel a harmonious peace, to have things somehow neatly in equilibrium. The truth is, most of us do not have balanced chemistries, smooth relationships, functional families, or stay in a constantly happy state for very long. We deal with mood cycles, hormones, family tensions, unexpected news, rocky relationship cycles, and the human tendency to be frustrated with ourselves and others. Our hearts and minds get saturated with stress, and it's often a real task to maintain a positive outlook or sense of balance in the face of turmoil.

The paradoxes of living are endless. Happiness can come in powerful doses, along with tremendous grief. "Good" or "bad" news can often be bundled together. One day, we may be overjoyed; on the next, heartbroken. We're constantly faced with the challenge of managing this jolting roller coaster called "life."

Years ago, we used to think that a sense of "imbalance" signaled something dreadfully wrong. But the latest statistics show that one in four of us deals with some form of anxiety and depression.

It's important to remember that we are constantly going through stages as we try to adapt and make sense of the intense joy and heartache that often face us simultaneously. We no longer think of struggle as a fixed state but as something we can go in and out of during different phases of our lives. Often, we are working through many of layers of complexities. We deal with the tensions of the day-to-day—the running around, the to-do list, and whatever curveballs we're thrown. Then, whether we know it or not, we are constantly managing those things that are deeply embedded in our minds, like strained family dynamics, hurts, and issues in self-acceptance and self-confidence.

True "balance" is usually elusive, considering what we are up against. Finding balance is less about being in some sort of Zen zone than it is about *accepting the inevitable highs and lows.* Sometimes the balance is in working at really enjoying the good moments, appreciating their wonder, and realizing just how special they are.

When bad moments hit, balance can involve working to try to "buy time," realizing that life will get better eventually.

> **Bottom Line:** The predominant view of "balance" is often a fallacy that leaves us searching for some mythical version of harmony or a peaceful state that just might not be possible given life's pushes and pulls. A healthier attainment of balance comes in appreciating the pleasant moments and riding out the tough ones.

Chasing rainbows

Other aspects of golden-ticket thinking include the "grass is greener" view that makes us feel that our lives are boring, insignificant, or way more difficult than those of most people. We sometimes think that we are the only ones who work hard or struggle. From afar, it seems that others have it easier or better in some way or another. Looking at others in this way is a lot like window shopping—something looks enticing from a distance, but once you get up close, it may not be what you really want. Everyone has some form of complexity and struggle in their lives.

The irony of all these forms of wishful thinking is that, generally, when the big things we dream about finally happen, they're not always what they're cracked up to be. Sometimes the imagining and planning feel more exciting than when we reach the goal itself. As the song suggests, "it's the climb" that's gratifying, since "there's always going to be another mountain!" If you're like me, you may not even take the time to celebrate your accomplishments or stop and acknowledge the wonder of the view—because we're too focused on "finishing" or "getting there" or planning the next big expedition.

Wanting more helps us stay driven and focused, but it's important to keep our longings in check and to keep perspective. Becoming obsessed with reaching greener pastures may, indeed, interfere with all of the wonderful aspects of our lives that sometimes are overlooked or undermined by chasing rainbows. In this quest for "something better," we can end up forgetting to appreciate what we have.

I know a couple who bought an exclusive piece of property in an elite part of town purely for status, even though it was well beyond their means. They sank their life's savings into it and spent years obsessively working to build the ultimate dream home. In the meantime, they lived in squalor in a tiny condominium with barely enough food or resources for survival. They sacrificed having the provisions they needed for their family to thrive over the years. Every ounce of effort went toward building this grand home. After their family was raised, the dream finally came to fruition.

It was heartbreaking to see the level of fragmentation and dysfunction that existed in the family by the time the home was built. Indeed, the parents' dream of greener pastures was realized, but at the expense of many people. Their new home ended up being a metaphor for neglect and greed rather than a source of pride and enjoyment.

We can all learn something from this extreme example. Being hyperfocused on our future dreams can lead us to miss, and even destroy, the critically important things in our present lives.

> **Bottom Line:** Dreaming big and reaching goals can be exhilarating. At the same time, it's important to find ways to appreciate what we already have, enjoy the process, and stay grounded in our pursuits. We may detour from our happiness if we are too focused on something that seems to offer promise but may end up being antithetical to our dreams when we arrive.

Dissect and Reflect

- What are my golden tickets, the things I wish for and believe will bring me great happiness?
- Are there things that I already have that I do not appreciate enough?

- In what ways has counterfactual thinking affected me?
- What versions of regret do I wrestle with?
- Is there anything I can do to slow down and enjoy the process more, while still realizing the goals I aspire to?
- Am I consumed with thinking that the grass is greener elsewhere? If so, what aspects of my life are worth appreciating more?

Chapter 5 in a Nutshell
There's no golden ticket

1. **Waiting for the big break**
   - Golden tickets are a universal draw, compelling us to believe that some "big break" will set us free.
   - We pine for relational, financial, and career breakthroughs to deliver us from our dissatisfaction.
   - Magical thinking tricks us into believing that we will be much happier "if only" something else happens or exists.
   - We return to our general level of happiness whether something exhilarating or atrocious happens.

2. **"More" doesn't equal "happy"**
   - We are bombarded with constant messages enticing us into thinking that the "perfect" car, house, face, or body will make us more fascinating or legitimate.
   - The effort to attain impossibly perfect "Hallmark moments" is another kind of pressure; however, life's joys are often found in the unplanned events.
   - Modern-day trappings can undermine our confidence and contentment.
   - The quest for success can propel us to overwork and to underappreciate what we have.

3. **What if?**
   - Counterfactual thinking leads to constant second-guessing and rumination.
   - It's difficult to acknowledge just how little control we often have.
   - Regret is a common human struggle.
   - Including "other" factors in our understanding of decisions and events helps us manage regret and other thoughts about loss.

- Factors like time and place, available resources, developmental state, personal traits, health factors, accidents, and outside influences beyond our control will have a tremendous impact on life outcomes.
- Jeanne and Ronaldo teach us that counterfactual thinking is truly a slippery slope.

4. **The myth of balance**
   - "Balance" is often elusive in the face of life's paradoxes.
   - Relationships, moods, family tensions, and unexpected news can disrupt our sense of balance.
   - Sometimes balance is more about enjoying the good things and riding out the storms than finding a mythical "Zen zone."

5. **Chasing rainbows**
   - The-grass-is-greener mind-sets make us feel isolated, dissatisfied, and envious.
   - We can easily forget to "enjoy the climb."
   - Chasing rainbows can take away from seeing the existing beauty around us.
   - Dreaming big about greener pastures is a healthy part of life that also requires a level of satisfaction with "what is" already.

6

CALM TREES

Reject your sense of injury and the injury itself disappears.
—Marcus Aurelius

> ESSENTIAL QUESTION:
> What forms of hardship have shaped you most?

I'll have some resilience, please.

Hurricanes are notorious for uprooting things, but palm trees remain intact even at intense wind velocities. Because of their composition and structure, they are able to withstand long stretches of nature's wrath and bend to the point of nearly touching the ground without snapping. Science has demonstrated that massive storms actually promote growth for these trees, strengthening the root system.

One breed in particular, known as hardy palm trees, are known to withstand even the coldest and harshest conditions. You could say that these trees are indeed calm in the face of a storm.

Nature makes us Resilient

What about people? Is there something inherent in our design, as well? Psychological "hardiness" has been discussed as a part of personality that helps us stay healthy even when we encounter major bumps.[46] Hardy people seem to find a way to bounce back from adversity.

Term	Definition	Consider This
Hardiness	Capacity for enduring or sustaining hardship; being able to survive under unfavorable conditions.	Like palm trees and other forms of nature, humans are hardy capable of growth and repair even after being bent down by life's storms.

A new concept has taken the theory of hardiness a few notches further in our understanding. Google the word "resilience"—you'll see a boatload of books, studies, and people talking about it.

---

[46] Suzanne C. Kobasa and her team at the University of Chicago brought this construct into the limelight in 1979.

Lots of human behavior folks and brain researchers[47] who have broken new ground in our understanding of personality have put a lot of effort into exploring what makes people resilient, especially given the confusion arising when people in almost identical situations have widely different reactions to stress.

What is it exactly that keeps someone going, while others seem flattened by life's curveballs? How can Bette, who grew up in a chaotic home environment, go on to become the CEO of a company and her brother Danny end up addicted to drugs? Like many, Bette worked her way through her disadvantages, developing a thick skin and learning needed coping strategies that translate well in the corporate world. Instead of those early difficulties crushing her, she was able to develop a strong will and sense of perseverance.

Lots of people are marveling at this type of capacity. For instance, Malcolm Gladwell, in his latest installment of thought-provoking prose, asserts that disadvantages can indeed be advantages, for they force us to think outside of the box and craft creative strategies for survival and success. In his book *David and Goliath*, he asserts that our notions of underdogs and struggle are often backward and that it is often because of difficulties, not in spite of them, that we are able to reach our goals. Talk about making the most of our stress!

Resilience is about grit, adaption, and determination. If you've faced a crisis of any magnitude, it's likely that you've asked yourself, *What is the point of all this?* Most of us are inclined to think such thoughts when life has knocked the wind out of our sails. But we're starting to learn more about what helps us press on, even when recovery doesn't at first seem possible.

Studies of resilience suggest that nature has provided powerful protective mechanisms that drive us to meet our basic needs for connection, belonging, and meaning. These instincts have little to do with what we look like, where we're from, where we live, or how much money we have—leaving room for people across a wide range

---

[47] Check out the work of Bruce McEwen, PhD. The author of over six hundred peer-reviewed articles, Dr. McEwen offers a multitude of windows into understanding of the influence of stress and resilience on health and illness.

of perspectives and circumstances to eventually regain momentum even when things initially look so unpromising.

Resilience is indeed dynamic and complex. It can take on different forms, ranging from the intensive "let me back in the ring," eye-of-the tiger mind-set to the more subtle "Everything's going to be all right," one-day-at-a-time mind-set. A hallmark feature of resilience is being subjected to some form of adversity and eventually being able to adapt once the stressor is relieved and basic needs are restored. Here's more on that:

Term	Definition	CONSIDER THIS
Resilience	A process involving positive adaptation in the face of significant adversity.	Despite being walloped, the resilient person eventually adapts and continues forward toward growth and healing. Adversity can force us to think in new ways and problem solve with a sense of intensity and urgency that helps us meet our goals.

The new school of thought says that everyone is born with innate resilience and that our capability to develop such resilience is quite monumental—a bit contrary to early beliefs about which factors were the most important determinants in shaping a person. Experts have spent a ton of time attempting to pinpoint the X factor that leads to success, well-being, and positive outcomes. More than ever, we're realizing that the presence of struggle actually affords us the opportunity to build emotional muscle. This sounds logical, but how can we make it possible? When we stop and evaluate how we are interpreting struggle, it allows us to harness our strengths and move forward in powerful ways. This often hinges on how we are making sense of things before, during, and after we are clobbered with something challenging. We'll talk more about this in chapter 9, "Energize."

Take (at least) two

Movie directors know that their first take isn't necessarily the best, and so they shoot multiple takes to capture the desired scene. The same is true when it comes to building resilience through our first and second "takes" on what is happening and how we can respond.

One proven aspect of strengthening our root systems involves a process known as "appraisal." Appraisals help distinguish the value or significance of something, and we often think of them as being associated with a prized possession, like a ring or antique. With regard to our thought processes, primary appraisals can be thought of as our "first take"—when we're first presented with bad news, a particular problem, or some form of hardship. Primary appraisals are usually messy, invoking intensive and raw emotion. When we're first clobbered with stress, this first stage of coping is usually overpowered with negative emotions and thoughts. You'll learn more about this in the "Realize" section of RESET.

Term	Definition	Consider This
Primary appraisal	Our "first look" at problems or situations. During this phase, it's often difficult to see possibilities and options because we're inundated with such thoughts and reactions.	Having a positive reaction to stress when it first arises is counterintuitive. It takes time to make sense of things before we can regroup and start the process of problem solving.

Resilience experts have started to zoom in on what happens following the primary appraisal. Once the dust has settled and emotions have calmed down a bit, the "second take" or secondary appraisal has a chance to come into play. Secondary appraisals allow us to revisit the source of stress and consider what can be done about it. In this stage of coping, we're more likely to be able to see the big picture, problem solve, and maintain a sense of hope that is stronger than when we were first flooded with whatever tensions arrived at our doorstop.

Term	Definition	Consider This
Secondary appraisal	Our "second look" at problems or situations. During this phase, it becomes more likely that we can begin problem solving and regrouping.	Being able to put our problems against a bigger backdrop can prove incredibly helpful. This stage allows us to see the resources we have to move forward.

When problems first come up, they can evoke some pretty messy thoughts. How can we best respond to raw emotion? Being saturated with these initial feelings is anxiety provoking and plain miserable, leaving the best of us sidelined. Problem solving requires a certain measure of savvy and a blend of optimism and realism. It requires us to look at the big picture and determine what is actually working *well.* The tendency to look at what's wrong, broken, or flawed can lead to our stalling out when it comes to working through problems of all sorts. At first, problems may seem insurmountable, but after reappraisal, our anxiety lessens, and we are better equipped to tackle what's at hand.

Part of this involves making meaning of what is happening. In fact, being able to uncover meaning and draw upon resources goes a lot further than avoiding stress. If we're actively aware of our process of "first and second takes," we can coach ourselves to figure out why something is happening, leading to important discoveries about what can be done about it.

Problem solving is another important aspect of resilience. Problems are an inevitable part of life, and both *expecting them* and *expecting to be able to solve them* help prevent us from getting deflated for too long in the face of stress. When we do not anticipate problems, we end up derailed and stuck, creating barriers to coping. At the same time, focusing too much on what could go wrong is an impediment to problem solving. In such moments, it can be helpful to reflect upon whether you or someone you know has encountered and overcome a similar obstacle. If so, thinking about the steps and strategies involved may provide a framework for coping and pressing forward.

Term	Description	Consider This
Problem solving	Involves planning, seeking help, critical/ creative thinking, imagining various possibilities, and developing needed strategies toward resolving a problem or minimizing its impact.	When we work at being nimble, strategic, focused and multidimensional, we become better equipped to understand both problems and potential solutions.

Bottom Line: Ask yourself: "Is this a solvable problem? Does this remind me of something I have encountered before?"

What we think about our ability to problem solve matters. If we hold the belief that we are capable, it contributes toward something known as "self-efficacy," which Albert Bandura made famous in the realm of social psychology. Self-efficacy beliefs directly impact our choices, especially when it comes to taking risks and making decisions.

Term	Definition	Consider This
Self-efficacy	Belief in one's own sense of agency or capabilities in relationship to setting and meeting goals.	If we believe that we have the facility to get something done, we are more likely to set and accomplish goals.

High self-efficacy frames our thinking. If we believe in our capabilities, we're more likely to roll up our sleeves and get fired up about challenges before us, wanting to master them. Rather than seeing challenges as obstacles, self-efficacy helps us to see them as puzzles to be solved, spurring us on in creativity. These beliefs and behaviors help build stamina and resilience.

BOTTOM LINE: If we feel efficacious, we are more likely to develop ambitious strategies and take the necessary steps to make things happen. When we have high self-efficacy, we feel capable and esteemed, ready to take on new challenges, even when there is a risk in doing so.

Resilience also involves our sense of independence. While connection to others is vital, is also known to be a contributing force in resilience. Autonomy allows us to separate ourselves from negativity and "groupthink" that may get in the way of coping. Feeling competent and able to carry out our roles and responsibilities without needing high levels of support can bolster self-confidence. This of course relates to how we define "independence" and involves the cultural context in which we've been socialized. Autonomy allows us to contribute toward a group's goals but keep our own ideas and resources handy.

Term	Definition	Consider This
Autonomy	Sense of identity, self-efficacy, self-awareness, task mastery, and adaptive distancing from negative messages and conditions.	Being able to set boundaries in relationships and avoiding codependency; feeling confident, competent; avoiding unhealthy relationships and being able to stand up for needs all contribute towards resilience.

While autonomy is important, making and building resilience doesn't happen in isolation. In fact, our connections, whether friends or family, are incredibly valuable. The people in our lives can cheer us on and act like a glue when we feel fragmented. Strong ties help us stay grounded and remind us to press on. When we have caring people in our lives, we benefit immensely. Few of us can muster up the courage and strength to keep a healthy outlook without some measure of support from those we love. They help us believe that we can, even during trying moments when our instincts first tell us otherwise.

Faith, fumbles, and fun

The tension between psychology and spirituality has long existed. However, the frameworks are much more similar and complementary than many imagine. While the tendency to separate both worlds has persisted in some ways, there's been a push to integrate our various sides in our understanding. Research is affirming that people who believe in God, or in a higher power outside of themselves, tend to have better emotional and even physical health. Faith is increasingly being seen as an important ingredient in resilience.

Having faith in God or a higher power leads to a greater sense of purpose and optimism. Faith helps us to look at the big picture and continue striving toward serving others, accomplishing personal goals, believing things will turn out well, and seeing beyond ourselves. Faith directly affects our optimism and belief in human good and redemption. It also helps us to understand our limitations and realize that the universe is not in our control. Faith often emphasizes that there is a reason for everything. Thinking about this when we're neck deep in stress can be very comforting. It allows us to stay hopeful and optimistic, even when there seems to be no end in sight of problems or hard work.

Speaking of optimism, kids laugh three hundred times a day on average. Adults—three! Really? The old adage "if you can't laugh, you'll cry" may indeed contain an important truth. With children, laughter abounds. As we age, our sense of humor tends to dwindle amid the problems of adulthood. If you find yourself rarely laughing at the inconsistencies and idiosyncrasies in your own life, this is an indicator that a dose of laughter is in order. If you do not crack up laughing regularly, you may end up "cracking up" in a way that wouldn't be so funny. As comedian Bob Hope once put it, "I have seen what a laugh can do. It can transform almost unbearable tears into something bearable, even hopeful."

The everyday, random quirks of our lives are often entertaining. The show *Seinfeld* was epic because of the fact that so many people could relate to the constant upheavals and random connections in daily living. The show exposed plenty of irreverent moments when the gravity of a situation (for some reason) strikes us as funny. I have had many of my own "*Seinfeld* moments," and realizing them as such has made stressful times more tolerable. Generally, annoyances eventually morph into a funny story, even though they may not have seemed so entertaining at the time they were unfolding.

DISSECT AND REFLECT

In order to prevent succumbing to locking down in adult mode, resorting to some "childish" behavior might just lighten your load. Consider the following:

- How often do I laugh, and over what?

- How seriously do I take myself?
- Am I spending time with others who make me laugh?
- What is the funniest thing that has ever happened to me?
- Do I live my life as though laughter is really the best medicine?

Studies show that that laughing is good for your health. When you laugh, you benefit in countless ways, including

- stronger immune system;
- increase in oxygen, endorphins, and serotonin (brain chemicals related to emotions);
- lower risk of heart problems and high blood pressure;
- connection with others;
- elevations in energy; and
- improved coping with stressors you are facing.

> **Bottom Line:** Health problems associated with stress are no joke. So laugh heartily, and know that in doing so, you are seriously improving your emotional and physical well-being.

The combination of acknowledging our humanness along with our spirituality and vulnerability can be liberating. When we recognize our wonder and limits and live for something beyond ourselves, we become more resilient. Being able to acknowledge, accept, and even chuckle at our limitations brings a great deal of relief. One of my favorite song lyrics from the Indigo Girls sums this up perfectly: "The best thing you've ever done for me is to help me take my life less seriously; it's only life, after all."

Chapter 6 in a Nutshell
Calm Trees

1. **I'll have some resilience, please**
   - Hardy palm trees and people have the capacity to strengthen roots during storms.
   - Our understanding of resilience has evolved, helping us pinpoint protective mechanisms that help us cope.
   - Resilience propels us to adapt and regain momentum when facing adversity.

2. **Take (at least) two**
   - Our "first take" is known as a "primary appraisal" and is usually raw and unfiltered.
   - Our "second take" is known as a "secondary appraisal" and is more rational and resource oriented.

3. **I think I can**
   - Over time and under certain circumstances, problems are often solvable.
   - "Self-efficacy" determines our readiness to take on new challenges.
   - Autonomy helps build initiative and confidence.

4. **Faith, fumbles, and fun**
   - It helps to believe that things will get better and that there's a reason for everything.
   - Acknowledging vulnerability can relieve us from thinking that we have control over all that happens in life.
   - Laughing at life's bloopers can go a long way.

PART 2

Moving toward Well-Being: The Five RESET Principles

෯ One Size Doesn't Fit All ๖

෯ Realize ๖

෯ Energize ๖

෯ Soothe ๖

෯ End Unproductive Thinking ๖

෯ Talk it Out ๖

7

ONE SIZE DOESN'T FIT ALL

Healthy citizens are the greatest asset that any country can have.
—Winston Churchill

> ESSENTIAL QUESTION: Which self-care
> strategies work best for you?

Cookie-cutter formulas don't cut it

Different things affect people differently. Being able to reset isn't
about following a prescribed, cookie-cutter formula but carefully
considering what tends to work best for you.

We all have a wide range of tastes, aptitudes, preferences, and
circumstances, right?

You could be repulsed by a restaurant or movie that I absolutely
adore. This is all part of the wonder of being human. For beach lovers,
being seaside is an absolute treat. For those who don't like it, the
experience is far from pleasant. Everyone has a different take on the
sensory experience generated from the sun, sand, and waves.

Along with our sensory perspective, the events of our lives—our
own unique histories—shape our beliefs, feelings, and how we see
the world. The people we've encountered and are in relationships

with have a major impact us. Few of us operate in pure isolation, so inevitably, our interactions are very much a part of a complex pattern that is fluid and constantly changing based upon the actions of those in our immediate and surrounding circles.

We're also at different points of our development. I could be struggling with something that seems completely benign to you. Life brings on certain types of challenges during its various stages. On top of that, we can be hit with whammies of all shapes and sizes that can require some serious effort toward restoration.

We all bring a variety of personal circumstances to the table, driving the amount of time and energy we can devote to self-care. We have unique demands, health factors, levels of energy, and support systems. Our conditions are vastly different. Some of us are enduring excruciating seasons of life, while others are challenged by bumps in the road. Either way, self-care is important. It's not about being a rock star when it comes to coping with stress but staying nimble in terms of how you are responding to what's at hand. Wherever your starting stress point is, the goal is to move that starting line as far as possible and to get you going forward in a positive direction.

Human capital matters

Society has a terrible track record when it comes to trying to prescribe a one-size-fits-all approach to life. This contributes to isms of all sorts, including racism, sexism, classism, heterosexism, ageism, and ableism. Unfortunately, snap judgments and prescriptive categorizing can quickly lead to the ugly world of stereotyping, discrimination, and oppression. Historically, dominant groups have tried to define what is "normal" or "acceptable," while leaving anyone falling outside such definitions as "less than" or "broken." This type of categorizing leads to disastrous consequences, inhibiting human potential and promise.

Term	Definition	Consider This
Oppression[48]	When prejudice and institutional power combine forces, they create a system that discriminates against certain "target" groups, while benefitting other "dominant groups."	Oppressive "isms" are reflected individually and institutionally through values, beliefs, feelings, actions, behaviors, language, rules, policies, procedures in society—harming all of us.

Oppression is a powerful force, exerted consciously and unconsciously by those holding privilege in society. With certain social groups having more value and power ascribed to them, others are devalued and marginalized. Our mental health and well-being hinge on this. In addition to health disparities,[49] there are many additional consequences of favoring certain members of society and damaging others. Given the despicable history of our country with regard to human rights and equality, it is no wonder that we continue to see such terrible gaps in social justice and human well-being. Unfortunately, there is a lot of yelling and polarization happening politically and in the media that prevents us from getting to a place of thinking collectively about how to harness human potential moving forward.

---

[48] Joe Feagin, US sociologist and social theorist's book Systemic Racism offers an in-depth analysis of oppression and racism impacting our societies.

[49] The Robert Wood Johnson Foundation has some extraordinary examples of the latest research devoted to uncovering disparities and making them known to promote needed changes.

Term	Definition	Consider This
Privilege	Operates on various levels and gives advantages, favors, and benefits to members of dominant groups at the expense of members of target groups.	Privilege relates directly to power. "Power over" is seen within our structure for human relationships and is detrimental on many levels.

One of the terrible consequences of isms and oppression is the significant and harmful disparities seen within our country and across the globe. When oppression and prejudice prevent people from having access to fundamental resources, they experience poor outcomes in physical and mental health, economic stability, educational attainment, incarceration rates, and more in comparison to those who have access to those resources.

BOTTOM LINE: In the United States, privilege has historically been granted to people with membership in one or more of the following social identity groups: white people, able-bodied people, heterosexuals, males, Christians, middle- or owning-class people, middle-aged people, and English-speaking people.

Isms hurt everyone, damaging our individual and collective power. When people are oppressed, it interferes with development of their fullest potential. Everyone is hurt by this, not just those in the marginalized group. Think of what would happen if all of the energy devoted toward hatred were harnessed and used for the greater good! Fortunately, increased attention is being devoted to the notion of "human capital": being able to leverage the assets of people to promote greater value within an organization or society. Considering the amount of work to be done in building a better world, it seems that working to support the needs and well-being of every member of society could have a tremendous impact. Imagine what could be accomplished if this were the case!

Term	Definition	CONSIDER THIS
Human capital	Collective skills, knowledge, and assets of people that are a value to organizations and society.	By leveraging human resources, we are bringing out the best in all people, allowing them to reach their fullest potential.

Thankfully, demographic changes and globalization are getting people to reject these longstanding, pervasive notions of privilege and superiority and increase their level of what Richard Bucher calls "diversity consciousness." This way of thinking can prove transformative. A major part of personal and societal well-being hinges upon individuals' working toward higher empathy through self-reflection and changing such terrible historic injustices, which are not only seen within groups of people, but—more destructive—are also entrenched in our institutional policies and practices.

Term	Definition	CONSIDER THIS
Diversity consciousness[50]	State of being that reflects understanding, awareness, and skills in the area of diversity.	Such skills as flexible thinking, communication, team work, and empathy are valuable both personally and professionally.

---

[50] While this is a textbook I use when teaching about diversity, it's very readable and worth picking up: Bucher, 2014, *Diversity Consciousness: Opening our Minds to People, Cultures and Opportunities*.

Raising consciousness and building diversity skills are powerful tools. It allows us to factor major historic influences into our awareness of ourselves and others. Instead of blaming individuals when they experience difficulties, it allows us to consider destructive circumstances that have an impact on them—and on us all—and how we may need to rethink how we interpret behavior.

Consider how our schools, medical establishments, and other institutions have framed human behavior. We tell students to "sit still" and listen and then label them when they're "out of line," without accounting for the fact that maybe they haven't had a proper breakfast or may be dealing with incredibly challenging obstacles. Or maybe they are plain bored from a lesson that seems irrelevant and drones on. Students are often blamed, rather than our evaluating the schools and larger systemic forces influencing the delivery of education.

> **BOTTOM LINE:** Forces in society can severely limit our growth and potential. Oppression and various "isms" hurt us all.

Out of the shadows

In December 2013, the White House announced its plan to "bring mental illness out of the shadows," with President Barack Obama stating:

> We know that recovery is possible. We know help is available, and yet, as a society, we often think about mental health differently than other forms of health. You see commercials on TV about a whole array of physical health issues, some of them very personal. And yet, we whisper about mental health issues and avoid asking too many questions.

RESET: Make the Most of Your Stress

This new campaign,[51] along with ongoing efforts by the National Alliance for the Mentally Ill,[52] (NAMI) and the World Health Organization (WHO) helps bridge the divide that has existed far too long surrounding mental health issues. The more we realize that emotional turmoil is quite human and that getting help is far less scary than one may fear, the better off we are. We've got to stop putting the stamp of disapproval on ourselves or others during times of struggle and work to get to the bottom of things. For those who have endured any form of anxiety or depression, you know just how unsettling it is. Society's old attitudes toward getting help have caused too many people to miss out on the countless opportunities to feel better and enjoy a healthier, more satisfying life.

This all needs to be taken into consideration when developing your RESET plan. Perhaps you have encountered negative barriers or messages that have forced you to subscribe to a certain formula or dogma that has left you feeling like you have to hide or conform to be accepted and worthy. The complexity of societal functioning calls us to consider what works for us and how we want to carve out an authentic path that gives us the momentum to overcome labels, obstacles, and injustices that continue to take their toll on human well-being.

Tailor it

The RESET principles are designed to be adapted to your own needs. Because we are all so different, each component will require you to think about what makes the most sense given your own unique identity (gender, cultural, religious, etc.) and life circumstances. You will find that different moments will require a higher level of focus on certain elements over the others. Each of the five principles can be tailored based on your self-care needs. One size doesn't fit all, but

---

[51] www.mentalhealth.com contains various videos, stories, and resources to help engage the public in new ways of thinking about mental health.

[52] www.nami.org offers a wide range of materials and supports to dispel myths and encourage open dialogue and intervention.

the principles are flexible enough for us to be able to maximize our growth and potential with regular practice. The best part is, the more we use these principles, the more natural it will become to integrate them into daily routines. Over time, RESET will help you stay focused and consistent in doing things that protect your emotional well-being and help you recalibrate when you start to feel overwhelmed.

Dissect and Reflect

- What factors and circumstances impact my ability to cope (past and present)?
- How have I overcome past obstacles, and how do I plan to keep doing so?
- What do I need to continue working on in order to accomplish this?

Chapter 7 in a Nutshell
One Size Doesn't Fit All

1. **Cookie-cutter formulas don't cut it**
   - Our different tastes, aptitudes, and preferences call for a wellness strategy that steers clear of a cookie-cutter, generic, or prescribed formula.
   - Our different seasons of life and points in our development call us to implement unique strategies that work best for us.

2. **Human capital matters**
   - Discrimination and oppression hurt us all.
   - Our society's track record needs work in order for us to harness human potential.

3. **Out of the shadows**
   - National and global efforts are under way to reduce stigma and to promote parity in access to mental health.

4. **Tailor it**
   - The RESET principles help us craft a 24-7 self-care plan designed for our own needs.
   - Regular practice allows us to stay grounded as life storms strike.

8

REALIZE

Hope is the feeling you have that the
feeling you have isn't permanent.
—Jean Kerr

ESSENTIAL QUESTION: What kinds of triggers
tend to bring on the most stress for me?

Twinkle, twinkle, little nose

"Messy" was my middle name in my younger years. Unmotivated to pick up the trails I left around the house, I went through a full-fledged couch-potato phase, watching classic 1980s sitcoms with great zeal.

Being the clutter bug that I was, I was captivated by the main character in the series *Bewitched*, the housewife-but-really-witch, Samantha Stephens. With a mere scrunch of her nose, she would turn a disaster zone into a room that looked like something out of a Martha Stewart magazine. If only. My eyes were wide as I contemplated this. I couldn't help but be drawn into the lure of the magical instant fix.

We all pine for immediate solutions when it comes to life's challenges. Just like when someone hits your knee, it jerks—when life's messes strike, you instinctively want to clean them up.

Unfortunately, the very moment our brain is inundated with the message that "something is wrong" is also the very moment that we are least equipped to problem solve. While we reflexively scramble to try to figure it all out, our knee-jerk reactions to stress are usually wrong since we haven't had time to confer with the parts of our brain known for judgment, reasoning, and processing. With no time to digest what's at hand, we blame, overanalyze, and act irrationally. We can drive ourselves (and maybe everyone around us) crazy. In the throes of distress, it's not necessarily the best time for an in-depth analysis of our lives, but that's precisely where we tend to gravitate.

During these stuck moments, it is necessary to take a step back and regroup before picking up and problem solving. We can call this "buying time," "regrouping," "calming down," or "thinking it through." Those old count-to-ten methods may not have been the worst idea, but if you're like me, you need more than ten seconds to come to your senses.

Finding ways to coach ourselves can help us counteract the range of emotional states triggered by stress. The RESET principles are designed to help in all kinds of difficult moments; I know from experience that the more we use them, the less likely we are to find ourselves in emergency mode. In other words, even when we find ourselves saturated in stress, we'll be better equipped to cope. Doing this may not be as simple as Samantha's magical solutions, but over time, we'll develop a sense of being more grounded and flexible, even when we're dealing with complicated people and problems.

The first principle in **RESET** is **R**EALIZE

"I've learned never to make a decision when I have PMS!" explained Naomi, a friend of mine. I was twenty-three at the time and always appreciated the simplicity and depth of her wisdom. Since then, I have extended this to "I never make decisions when I am tired, lonely, frustrated, overworked, sick ..." I also try to refrain from making day-to-day decisions or blanket judgments about the state of my life when I am clearly wound up or wiped out.

The importance of *realizing* what is going on with ourselves cannot be overstated. Clinically, we call this "reflection," "developing insight," "self-awareness," or "perspective taking." This happens in the "secondary appraisal" phase of coping, discussed in chapter 6, "Calm Trees." Taking inventory once we've had enough time for our raw emotional responses to recede can serve as a springboard toward well-being. Sometimes this takes a few moments—and other times much longer. Either way, it's important to carve out the time needed to do so. Being able to reflect on what is happening and how we are responding can be a huge help in coping with very dark emotions and trying moments.

Those aha! reflective moments are pivotal—when insight happens and leads you to stop blaming yourself or others. It helps us zoom in on what may be adding fuel to the fire and how this is impacting our stress thresholds. We all have triggers that ramp up our stress. As we've learned, it's what we *believe* about their impact that can either leave us stuck or propel us into positive feelings and action.

For example, I may have a deadline looming, which comes with a certain measure of stress that is needed to help me complete the task. Yet I've learned that certain triggers can tip the balance and send me into a state of uncertainty. These triggers can relate to something even as simple as the time of the day, when my mind may be full from the day's events. Knowing this, I realize that late night isn't the best time to dissect whether or not I will be able to complete a project. With this more rational understanding, I then have to convince myself that it is unproductive to waste time and energy stewing. The natural anxiety of a deadline is trumping reason, and I remind myself to trust the process, that I am capable of completing the work—and that, in order to do so, what I really need is a good night's sleep. This process relies on what is known as "self-talk," which is a fancy way of naming the coaching process that we can use to regain traction during slippery moments.

This type of insight helps us to dip into our mental reserves and tackle what's at hand from a fresh perspective. We may need something simple to help us get our bearings. We might need food or water in our systems, a brisk walk, a laugh with a friend, or a catnap to help tune our systems. Things like low blood sugar, dehydration, being stuck in serious mode, and feeling tired tax not only our physical health but also our emotional well-being. We'll cover more of this ground in chapter 10, "Soothe."

> **Bottom Line:** Our knee-jerk reactions to stress impede our ability to problem solve and reason. When we're in this state, it's best to *realize* it and wait until we're ready to take a second look at what we're facing and what, realistically, can or cannot be done.

Reframing trumps blaming

Our gut reactions often have a blaming element directed toward ourselves or others. Often, our automatic response to stress leads us to focus on shortcomings. It takes effort to work toward reframing our first reactions. Reframing involves looking at the big picture and identifying something more positive to hold onto. Some examples include:

Blame versus Reframe	
Blame	**Reframe**
I'll never be able to handle tomorrow's day ...	I've done it before, and if I get a good night sleep, I'll feel better about it then.
I'm lazy, and I don't have the energy for my run ...	Maybe this cold is affecting me more than I realized. Once it passes, I'll be back on the trails again.

I hate my job. People are curt and inconsiderate. No one will stop to spend more than two minutes in a conversation ...	This is our busy time of year, and everyone's nerves are frayed. Lots of people are curt, but not everyone. When we make it to the end of the quarter, things will loosen up.
I'll never find someone who understands me. I'm going to end up permanently alone ...	Right now, I'm struggling after a tough breakup. Even though I'm lonely, this is probably a good time to heal and figure out what I want in my next relationship. If I rush into something too quickly, maybe I'll make a decision that I'll regret.

Reframing is tricky when we're in certain modes that instantaneously raise adrenaline, making for a real challenge. Our bodies secrete hormones, such as cortisol—which is, in fact, an important mechanism designed to help our systems respond to threats but is problematic when too much of it floods our bodies.

BOTTOM LINE: Reframing helps us to stop and realize what is increasing our emotional disarray. It helps us remember to look at the context of our lives and put necessary structures in place that maximize our resources—both internal (like reasoning, coping, and humor) and external (like helpful information, people, and activities).

Sanjay's story

Take Sanjay, for example. His adrenaline levels, triggered by a major blow, sent him into a tailspin. For the past fifteen years, he had worked his way up the ladder in his organization, only to find himself among the droves of workers being abruptly laid off. His family depended upon his paycheck, and he was anxious to secure something to stave off financial ruin.

After several promising interviews, the wait increasingly felt like forever. Late one night, following a marathon resume-posting bender, Sanjay's mind began to spiral out of control. His anxiety was palpable, and his thought process was as uncontrolled as a wildfire.

Despite having a certain measure of self-confidence, Sanjay was inundated with anxiety and found it impossible to reel his negative thoughts back in. He was at the pinnacle of panic.

Hours passed, and Sanjay finally got some needed rest. In the morning, he was able to taper the raw emotions with some reasoning. His circumstances were still unnerving, but he wasn't ruminating with such intensity. It dawned on him that the night was a tough stretch for him. He decided to change up his routine a bit so that he wouldn't stew so much. For one, he decided to end his online time by 9:00 p.m. and transition with a hot shower, cup of tea, and discussion with his wife, Jana, that was completely unrelated to the search process.

BOTTOM LINE: Uncertainty about what's to come can be harder to swallow than actual bad news. The unknown can be brutal, stretching our patience to new levels. When we're awaiting a decision, especially on major life events like health diagnoses, employment, college acceptance, and the like, our nerves can easily become frayed.

We all have peak anxiety moments. For some of us, it happens when the day is ending and we start looking ahead. For others, it hits in the mornings when we're gearing up to tackle our to-do lists. Many people have shared with me over time that Sunday nights are particularly anxiety provoking. The weekend is over, and the thought of the upcoming week brings on a sense of impending dread. Identifying which times of day, days of the week, seasons of the year, and stages of life that seem to be the most challenging helps us understand what may be triggering more intensive emotions. Knowing this can make our self-talk more targeted. We can remind ourselves that the way we feel is a temporary state related to such factors and that we'll eventually return to a more calm and rational place.

Sometimes it's difficult to pinpoint what is adding fuel to our fire. We often unconsciously make snap judgments or decisions based on our "gut reactions" that may not be as spot-on as we often believe they are. Daniel Kahneman and Amos Tversky's[53] work illustrates this. As a research team, they've spent years exploring how cognitive biases and unconscious reasoning can impact our perceptions. In *Thinking, Fast and Slow,* Kahneman asserts that we are often flat-out wrong when it comes to our judgments. We often make mistakes because of emotional reasoning, and our perceptions about ourselves and various situations can be dreadfully inaccurate.

> **BOTTOM LINE:** When you are tired, overworked, sick, full of adrenaline, or anticipating more stress ... it is not the right time for an *in-depth analysis* of your life! Instead, try to get unstuck by figuring out what triggered you and acknowledge it as an "off" moment, day, or season!

DISSECT AND REFLECT

- What influences my capacity for reasoning?
- What types of triggers tend to bother me?
- Am I spending too much time blaming myself or others?
- Think of two or three situations where I am caught in the trap of blaming. Can I identify a reframe in any of them?

---

[53] Unfortunately, Tversky passed away before the book's publication.

Chapter 8 in a Nutshell
Realize

1. **Twinkle, twinkle little nose**
   - The desire for a magical instant fix lures us into scrambling for immediate solutions.
   - When life gets messy, we want to instantly clean it up.
   - After being hit with something stressful, we often overanalyze and act irrationally.
   - Our knee-jerk reactions need to be tapered before we're ready to make sense of what's happening and begin problem solving.

2. **The first principle of RESET is REALIZE**
   - Identifying triggers helps us RESET.
   - Taking inventory helps us increase self-awareness.
   - Figuring out what fuels the fire helps us beef up our self-talk.

3. **Reframing trumps blaming**
   - Perspective is the springboard to well-being, catapulting us into developing structures to help us account for what we are facing.
   - Sanjay's unemployment history uncertainty was especially high at night, and small adjustments made a big difference in his ability to cope.
   - Our unconscious responses are not always rational (not even close!).
   - Self-care involves frequent reality checks, especially during peak anxiety moments.
   - Our gut reactions are often misinformed and inaccurate.

9

ENERGIZE

The best six doctors anywhere,
and no one can deny it, are sunshine, water,
rest and air, and exercise and diet.
—Wayne Fields, *What the River Knows*

ESSENTIAL QUESTION: Am I taking care of my
body in ways that suggest that I want to feel
my best?

Three short stories

Sallie Thompson wrestled with bouts of anxiety and
depression throughout her twenties, affecting her self-
esteem, work performance, and happiness. After reading
Thom Hartmann's *Walking Your Blues Away*, her neighbor
Beth suggested that she start walking, and before long,
Sallie felt a dramatic shift in her moods, energy, and
outlook.

As time went on, she decided to take it to the next
level and started mixing jogs into her routine. When she
came across a T-shirt with the slogan "Running is cheaper
than therapy" in her favorite local store, she couldn't

resist. Smiling to herself, she knew that she had found an important tool in her self-care regimen. She was thrilled that her investment was paying off in such a big way.

❧

Jana Greene's weakness was carbs. She constantly craved them and had a hard time resisting the urge, especially at work, where they were abundant in the community kitchen. In addition to packing on the pounds, Jana noticed her metabolism shooting downward.

Brent Garbo, who sat in the cubicle next to Jana, always had lots of spunk. He was constantly at the watercooler, crunching on apples, carrots, and nut bars. Jana asked Brent for some tips, and before long, she was inspired to eat more of what her body needed. Jana felt better, noticing a big improvement in her focus and stamina throughout the day.

❧

Fatima Burke impressed her friends with her resolve to work through her grief after her husband, Carlos, died from a heart attack following his routine morning run. The couple was well known for their zest for life and strong affinity for one another. They were constantly in motion, soaking up every experience possible, with others barely able to keep up. When Carlos died, everyone worried that Fatima would never be able to move forward.

Certainly, coping with what had happened was extremely difficult. At the urging of friends, Fatima immediately sought therapy to put a plan in place to help her manage. The first year was a blur in many ways, but Fatima was proud of her will, and she wanted to honor Carlos by moving forward and trying to rebuild her life. Some days were decent; others were disasters. Fatima stepped up her exercise and diet and also gave herself permission to take long naps when she needed to. Her body was on override, and the toll of the grief often left her reeling.

Although pleased with her progress, Fatima's therapist suggested that she consider going for massage. She pointed out that losing Carlos meant that she had also lost the daily physical touch she was used to. The daily hugs, snuggles, and intimacy were all things she missed very much, among many other aspects of their relationship. While she wasn't ready to become involved with someone, she recognized the power of human touch and decided to give it a try. Twice a month, Fatima made massage part of her self-care routine, which helped renew her system, giving her tremendous relief.

The second principle of RESET is ENERGIZE

Energizing is about invigorating our system with various forms of stimulation to refresh and renew. Our bodies respond to how we take care of them. A healthy blend of activity, consumption, rest, and human connection are cornerstone components of self-care.

Energizing involves four essential aspects:

1) **Movement:** The amount of physical activity we engage in
2) **Diet:** The types of food and drink we consume
3) **Rest and relaxation:** The amount of time we spent regrouping and sleeping
4) **Human touch:** Physical affection and intimacy, from hugs to the Big O

Energizing is about engaging in routines that bring about momentum and drive. If we deliberately invest in eating, workout, and sleep routines that support our metabolisms and body functioning, we're bound to feel better.

This is easier said than done, with a sedentary lifestyle leaving many of us sitting for long periods. Mix this with supersized helpings and quick-fix sugar, caffeine, and carb turbo-up remedies at every corner—and healthy energy levels become nearly impossible to sustain. This dreadful combination of inactivity and short-lived fuels leave most of us in serious need of a reset. Energizing is an essential piece of self-care that helps us recalibrate our systems and go the distance.

Move it!

We often equate working out with appearance. But there's so much more to gain from it. Exercise facilitates a wide range of helpful functioning in our brains and metabolisms, such as

- higher energy;
- reduced stress;
- smoother processing and reasoning; and
- improved focus, memory, and problem-solving capacity.

Who couldn't use some of that? Those who work out say that it's as much for their mental focus and emotional well-being as it is about fitting into their jeans. Sure, staying lean and mean is great incentive, but the mental and emotional health impact turn out to prove just as—or even more—highly rewarding.

Although the benefits of working out are far reaching, it's not easy to stay consistent with our routines. Time pressures, financial strains, injuries, illness, and boredom can all get in the way. Part of developing a realistic plan is to evaluate our own unique variables and set something up that is both feasible and sustainable for us individually. Once that happens, we can measure our progress, which is another vital component that supports follow-through.

Time crunches affect most of us, but the "I'm too busy to work out" justification won't get us too far. You may have noticed that even the most notoriously busy leaders often make the time to keep their brain and bodies in tune. The last few presidents have showcased their dedication to working out—Bill Clinton and George W. were joggers, and Barack Obama is an avid hoops player. First Lady Michelle Obama has also done a world of good showcasing her strength and promoting fitness and healthy eating.

When you think about the scale of their schedules, you realize that if the president and First Lady find time to exercise, then we can likely find space in our schedules to do so. They do it to stay healthy and sharp and to help counteract the enormous stresses they face. While we may not have the pressures of running a country, we still endure our own versions of extraordinary juggling between work and home. We need regular exercise to clear the junk out of our heads and bodies and maintain the impetus to keep going strong.

> **BOTTOM LINE:** If the president and First Lady can exercise, so can we. Even with a power-packed schedule, we can find time to invest in our health. If our schedules seem too busy for exercise, that's all the more reason we need it. The extra energy and stress-reducing effects will serve us well.

DISSECT AND REFLECT

Finding the time

Take a moment to sit with your schedule and highlight zones where working out is possible. Ask yourself:

- Do I have any time in the morning, midday, or late afternoon that works?
- Are there any particular days of the week that are more conducive to exercising than others?
- Is there anything to scratch off the list or rearrange in my schedule to make room for exercise?

Keeping costs in check

Besides limited time, money can seem like a barrier to exercising. But you don't necessarily need to join a gym to work out (and some gyms are much more reasonable in price than others). There're probably many possibilities right at your fingertips that you may not have noticed. In the "Recommendations for Further Growth" section at the end of this book, I give some additional suggestions on workout options, but for now, think about your current landscape and what you have access to.

- Are there parks or walking paths in the vicinity of work or home?
- Can I opt to take the stairs instead of my usual elevator ride?
- Is it possible for me to ride my bike to work or the store?
- Is there a pool open in my community?
- Can I park farther away to get some extra steps in the day?
- Do I have some small hand weights or household objects handy?
- Is there a friend or family member with whom it would be fun to walk or run?

Finding something you enjoy

In addition to thinking about proximity and ways to reduce costs, focus on activities that you are most drawn to. We often talk about finding work we love, since we spend so much time working. Likewise, we should find workout options that we really love so that we'll *want* to spend more time doing them. Often what we enjoy relates to what resonates well with our system. We are fanatical about certain types of exercise, because certain activities just seem to click for all of us in different ways. Even so, if you feel intimated because you're not confident about finding something you will like and do well at, by working at it, you will likely improve and eventually come to enjoy your new routine. It may take a few tries, but will be well worth it.

The latest trends, such as yoga, spinning, and interval training, are popular for good reason: each of these is an incredible way to reset our systems. In addition to the host of new trends, think about what you have typically enjoyed throughout your life. Did you ride a bike as a kid? Swim? Play a certain sport? If so, is there a way to bring that back into your routine now? Sometimes treadmills and classes just don't have enough appeal. Picking something we love helps prevent monotony. When we're bored or doing something we don't genuinely enjoy, the routines just won't stick. Just remember that it may take time for you to grow fond of your chosen activity.

Do any of these activities appeal to you?
• Swimming
• Biking
• Walking
• Yoga
• Golf
• Basketball
• Skating
• Jogging
• Kayaking
• Rebounding/trampoline
• Tennis
• Dancing
• Jump roping
• Spin classes
• Skiing/snowboarding

Learning what's possible

We all have different ages, aptitudes, and abilities. Even if you don't find yourself in great health or if you're experiencing obstacles, it's worth considering what *is* possible instead of focusing on what is *not*. Scan your environment and take inventory of what you are doing and what you might be able to add to your repertoire. Luckily, some great modifications exist for people of varying health circumstances and abilities. Some include chair or gentle yoga, swimming, stretching, and tai chi. Another go-to option is deep-diaphragm breathing. Never underestimate the power of deep breathing for reinvigoration. When rigorous workouts just aren't possible, remember that there are many breathing methods that contribute to increased oxygen and endorphins.

Stretching also has a lot of promise when it comes to clearing the body and mind. It's another powerful tool in the realm of self-care, helping us to energize our muscles through increased blood flow. This flow helps reduce stress and tension and, in turn, gives us higher energy. The icing on the cake is that it also decreases the risk of injury and helps improve athletic and day-to-day performance. Sounds like a worthwhile pursuit, doesn't it?

> **Bottom Line:** Picking the right activities and the right time and place to carry them out helps to ensure progress. Even if you are facing injury or illness or varying levels of ability, consider what *is* possible and what will work *best* for you.

Thinking about equipment

Contestants on *The Biggest Loser*[54] get the ultimate life reset, with resources for specialized coaching and meals taking them from the worst shape to the best of health. Their stories illustrate that change is possible; it shows us a wide variety of creative exercises, obstacle courses, and equipment to help with getting in better shape. This show is inspirational, as it demonstrates the power and possibility of changing even when things have seemingly gone past the point of no return. Since few of us have the great fortune of having trainers like Jillian, Bob, or Dolvett, we instead can borrow some of their nuggets of wisdom and introduce them into our lives in our own ways. One of the critical aspects of the show is the weekly weigh-in. Keeping track of our progress regularly and measuring what we are gaining and losing are essential.

Helpful devices

Last year, I started taking part in a pedometer program offered at work.[55] Every day, I faithfully clip on a pedometer and am surprised

---

[54] Few of us will make it onto the show, but *The Biggest Loser* has a lot of great programs and supports available. Check out its website for ideas and inspiration: www.biggestloser.com.

[55] Even if you don't have a pedometer, lots of health insurance companies offer them for free. Your local department store also keeps them stocked.

at how much it motivates me to track my progress. It tells me, "This week, you took more steps than 95 percent of the people in your organization!" It also tells me exactly how many steps I am racking up and how it compares with what others of my age and gender are doing. As simple as it seems, wearing the pedometer has influenced me to take the long route whenever possible and to get out for more runs and walks than ever. I've toned up and dropped a few pounds as a result. More than that, I feel an extra measure of pep to propel me through my very long list of responsibilities. I sometimes can't believe that that a mere black plastic circle could have so much influence, but it truly has.

Another handy tool is an app called Strava,[56] which I've taken to using on my runs. This has been another game changer in my self-care routines. I have it set to a British accent (which I am a complete fool for) and it gently reminds me after each half mile what my timing is. Even though I'm more of a jogger than a runner, my times have steadily improved. I chalk this up to my competitive spirit and am convinced that these measurement nudges are little fires being lit underneath me along the trails. After my runs, I get a report of what I've accomplished and little trophies. This little bit of positive reinforcement goes a long way, as does seeing some of my turtle moments (keeping me humble and striving to do better!).

Another great tool is Fitbit[57], which tracks activity, food, weight, and sleep. In addition to wristbands being available across many major stores, it also synchs well with electronic devices. This is an excellent way to measure progress and maintain motivation.

> **Bottom Line:** Measuring our activities gives us a realistic picture of our progress and helps inform our ongoing goal development. If we're not keeping track of what we're doing or not doing, it's very difficult to stay consistent in our efforts.

---

[56]   Check out www.strava.com for both foot and bike options.

[57]   See www.fitbit.com to learn more

Helpful clothes

Another very simple help with staying fit is to dress the part. There's something about putting workout clothes and sneakers on that can suddenly affect your mood and motivation. You feel more like an athlete, and this can go a long way. If you have to dress up for work or otherwise, you can keep sneakers in your car or office or in a packed gym bag that's ready to go. These simple strategies can set us up for success as we work toward healthy lifestyle improvements.

§

If you haven't been active for a while, this may all seem like a tall order. The key is to start with small, manageable goals and work from there. It takes time and persistence, but the built-in rewards soon create the momentum and drive you need to keep at it. Pick something that you can implement immediately, and commit yourself to this aspect of your self-care. See if you can enlist the support of someone else to help keep you on track. If you've worked out before, you are likely familiar with the feeling of not wanting to get started that is quickly overcome by a sense of gratification once you begin. In other words, even when we hate getting started, we feel great once we've finished a workout of any sort.

> **BOTTOM LINE:** You don't need to join a gym to work up a sweat for your RESET. Look at your current routines and what you have at your fingertips. Even as little as fifteen minutes a day can help you recalibrate. Getting the body moving and heart pumping is well worth your effort. Keep your sneakers on or with you at all times and look for opportunities to *move it!*

Dissect and Reflect

- Based on your evaluation of where you live and work, what opportunities will you take advantage of to fit in more movement?
- Can you pinpoint specific parts of the day that are conducive to taking a walk of any duration?
- Is there anyone around you who would make a great exercise partner?
- Do you own a pedometer or have apps to measure your workouts?

You are what you eat

Diet is the cornerstone of every facet of our health. We sometimes underestimate our diet's influence on our mental and emotional functioning. The phrase "you are what you eat" could be extended to "you feel as good as you eat." Just ask filmmaker Morgan Spurlock about his adventure with the fry guys. He underwent the ultimate health and human behavior experiment for his *Super Size Me* documentary, sacrificing any semblance of vitality for an entire month, as he endured a total McDonald's binge! In addition to the detrimental effect on his waistline after enduring thirty days of this burger-fries-soda-only diet, Morgan found himself with high blood pressure, low libido, and other markers of bad health, and he was dreadfully demotivated, depressed, and off-kilter.

Super Size Me is one of the most compelling examples of how diet can either bolster or zap our energy and health. The emotional, biological, and behavioral changes that Spurlock underwent in just a few short weeks were both shocking and persuasive. Even though most of us are unlikely to take on such an endeavor ourselves, we can learn a lot from his burger splurge.

A wealth of information about healthy eating is available to help us make choices that boost our mood and well-being. You can visit the Mayo Clinic's website, WebMD, or simply Google a topic to help you build your shopping list. Here are a few that I swear by:

- **Go bananas:** Seen as a perfect source of energy, bananas have long been known for their health- and energy-bolstering benefits. Bananas have been linked to boosting serotonin and helping regulate our blood sugar, moods, and more. Hey, while you're at it, an apple a day is also fantastic, and you can't go wrong with raw fruits and with veggies of all sorts.

- **Be grainy:** Quinoa, oats, popcorn, and brown rice are all awesome sources of nutrition. These whole grains, among a host of others, are getting a lot of attention for their ability to regulate our systems and provide lasting energy and balance for the body.

- **Chalk up the antioxidants:** Green tea, beans, berries, apples, baked russet potatoes, cherries, pomegranates, and artichokes are just a few of the many sources of antioxidants that can supercharge our immune system, prevent disease, help slow rapid aging, and keep us feeling nourished and fired up.

- **Drink up:** The idea that staying hydrated improves our health has caught on. Water has become the second most popular drink in America, and for good reason. Water bolsters our immune system and mood and helps flush out toxins, among other benefits. A popular recommended amount is 8 x 8, which translates to eight ounces (or one cup) eight times a day. Experts say that our water-drinking needs differ; in general, women need approximately two liters per day, while men need three liters per day. For some added ammunition, I love putting vitamin C packets into my water (once a day).

- **Lean protein machine:** Our energy levels can be directly linked to our protein consumption. When we eat fish, chicken, lean beef, tofu, eggs, ground turkey, eggs, and Greek yogurt, we're engaging in behavior that supports many facets of our health. Protein is known to help with emotional regulation and makes us stronger all around.

- **Omega-3:** Salmon, flax seeds, walnuts, and beans are just some of the foods loaded with essential fatty acids that are linked to heart health (both physical and emotional). There's a lot of discussion about the role of omega-3 in mood, memory, and learning.[58]

In addition to including certain foods in our diet, we want to avoid some, as well. Here are some major bad-health culprits that are often staples in American diets:

- **Caffeine:** Do we really run on it? For some, even small amounts of caffeine can lead to anxiety.
- **Salt:** Sodium slows us down, leaving our systems dried up, bloated, and at risk for problems like high blood pressure.
- **Alcohol:** Technically, alcohol is a depressant and can leave us flat if we're not careful. Overuse can negatively impact our brain, heart, liver, and immune systems.
- **Processed foods:** There's no shortage of these on our supermarket shelves. Watch out for unnatural products that contain dye and artificial ingredients that can lead to "brain fog," among other harmful consequences. They are also generally superpacked with sugars and fats.
- **Carbs:** Carbohydrates—breads, cereals, pasta, rice, sweets— are famous for overstimulating our dopamine levels, making us apt to crave more carbs for a quick fix. Carbs can satisfy initially but can tamper with our blood-sugar regularity, leading to difficulty with sustained energy and focus.

Often we don't realize that something we are eating or lacking in our diet is affecting our mood, energy, and health. It takes some troubleshooting to figure that out and is worth paying attention to. There are obvious culprits, like whopping amounts of caffeine or sugar, but a lot of others can fall below our radar screen without careful scrutiny. We sometimes crave things because our system

---

[58] Omega-3 supplements have become increasingly popular and can be highly beneficial. However, be aware that, for some people, too much omega-3 may not be a good thing. Listen to your body and check in with your health practitioner on whether your current diet alone is enough or whether a supplement would be a wise choice for you.

needs recalibration. Instead of discovering a way to truly reset, we sometimes give in and end up compounding our issues.

With food issues, we have to be alert so that we don't make matters worse for ourselves. This is especially important because, in addition to the food culprits we've mentioned, food sensitivities and allergies can seriously disrupt our systems.

Our household learned this lesson when our daughter, Tori, starting having upset stomachs and low energy levels. Our chiropractor, versed in nutrition, detected that she has a gluten sensitivity. This insight led us to cut out products with gluten (easier than it may seem) and, in just a few weeks, Tori felt like a new person. The results were written all over her face, which suddenly had a healthy glow and vibrancy we hadn't seen in a while. Even though she is not allergic to gluten, Tori's system was clearly agitated by it; by removing the problem, she experienced quite a transformation. Her results were so compelling that I decided to jump on the gluten-free bandwagon. Since I was already preparing her food and stocking the house accordingly, it was easy for me to join her. I haven't looked back since. I feel younger, healthier, and have even slimmed down a bit.

These results are common for those with sensitivities and allergies, but avoiding gluten may not necessarily be the exact change your system needs. It's worth connecting the dots between what you are eating and how you are feeling. Keeping a food journal for a few weeks is extremely informative if you're trying to pinpoint what makes you feel well and what doesn't.

It's also worth getting some feedback from the many people out there with this type of expertise. Whether you talk with primary care professionals or with other complementary practitioners (such as dieticians, nutritionists, acupuncturists, and chiropractors), you will benefit from discussion about your diet and your body's signals and symptoms. If you're not feeling your best, they will likely have some guidance around what you might do to get your system on track.

The stomach has been dubbed "our second brain" for good reason. Our guts contain more neurons than any other organ in our bodies besides our brains. Practitioners and researchers know that the stomach's ability to signal distress reveals our emotional and mental states. Having "butterflies" in the stomach is one illustration of this. Studies continue to demonstrate that the stomach not only receives messages from the brain but also sends them. If we're under a great deal of stress and eating poorly to boot, symptoms like acid reflux, irritable bowel syndrome (IBS), and constipation are our bodies' ways of signaling us to make some changes. IBS has been called the "mental illness of our second brains." Dr. Emeray Mayo, the director of the Center for Neurobiology of Stress at the University of California, asserts, "It's almost unthinkable the gut is not playing a critical role in mind states."

BOTTOM LINE: The combination of stress and poor diet can wreak havoc, and our stomachs are often the first to signal a problem. When we pay attention to the message our guts are sending, it helps keep our stress-management and healthy-eating efforts in the forefront of our self-care.

DISSECT AND REFLECT

Take a few moments to review what you've eaten over the past day or so. What have your meals, snacks, and drinks consisted of? What types of cravings do you experience? What did you notice you're already doing to eat well? Did you find any vices or bad habits? Based on this, identify:

- two to three new foods that you will add to your routines
- two to three foods that you plan to cut back on

Next, go directly to your cabinets and take inventory. Craft a grocery list that is packed with solid choices and avoids ones that get in the way of your RESET goals. You may need to clean out the tempting junk items that will sabotage your healthy decision making.

R³: Rest, Relax, Reflect

Research affirms the majority of us are sleep deprived, overstimulated, and unable to break away from the constant demands of work. I see evidence of this everywhere: in my colleagues, students, those who come to me for therapy, and certainly in my own life. To say that I'm a perfectionistic workaholic and a worrier would be a gross understatement. I ruminate about everything, and my schedule is borderline cruel. Just ask my friends and family. I am constantly working to manage my own level of stress brought on by nonstop demands and my proclivity toward seventy-plus-hour weeks.

Given the extremes in the economy and the increasing pressures inherent in our saturated, hypercompetitive market, it's often challenging to build in enough downtime to recharge our batteries. Pressures to perform academically, athletically, and otherwise have skyrocketed—now starting when children are very young. This carries right over into adult life, with massive competition for colleges, jobs, and financial security. This leaves many of us whipped up and forever burning the candle at both ends.

These days, most of us are likely to respond to the question "How are you?" by using the word "busy." Ned Hallowell reminds us of this in his *Crazy Busy* book. The wild rat race pace of today leaves us unlikely to shift down and relax. We end up feeling fraotic (a blend of frazzled and chaotic), and our adrenaline can easily turn to anxiety. It can leave us to wonder, *How did life get like this?*

When we consider our total health, our schedule is a big piece of the pie. The boundaries we set around our time are important to our health. How much we pack in directly relates to how much time is left to rest and regroup. There is such a thing as a healthy schedule. While crafting the "perfect" version of this may not be possible, some of the telltale features to consider include:

- **Transitions:** It's important that our schedules allow us some time to shift gears from work or whatever else demands our energy. Transition time helps put our minds at rest. Making time to unwind can go a long way.

- **Reflection:** Reflecting on what has happened and what's to come is a valuable process. We need to set aside time to think and make sense of things—alone and with others. When we reflect, it helps us cope, live thoughtfully, renew purpose, and gear up for what's ahead. Reflection facilitates working through our appraisal process, helping us to reframe and problem solve.
- **Play:** Healthy schedules include room to play, laugh, and be creative. If we're stuck in serious mode or only working, we can lose our imagination, sense of humor, and desire for adventure. These all make a huge difference in staying healthy and positive.
- **Sleep:** The ultimate reset, sleep works wonders and is needed for our brains and bodies to recalibrate and energize. When we're sleep deprived, we bring down our coping abilities a few notches and disrupt our motivation levels.

All of this may seem terribly unrealistic given the types of demands inherent in today's world. If you're like me, it's hard to say no to things, which leads us to a state of "no margins"—moving from one thing to the next with barely any time to regroup, process, or even think straight.

Being reasonably busy can be healthy and very satisfying. Too much downtime can lead to excessive thinking, lack of engagement, and low motivation—at times, even to a feeling of isolation and depression. Sometimes when we don't have a lot to do, tasks seem magnified because we have time to give them too much attention. When busy, we've already got a lot of momentum, and we may not feel that it's a big deal to add a few more things to the list. We may sometimes complain about all we have to do, but it's better than not having any responsibilities or not having the health and resources to get things done.

So being superbusy is not always a bad thing. It forces us to have to get everything done, with little room for procrastination. In fact, if you tend to be an overscheduler, you are apt to feel energized when there's lots of action and structure in your life. A certain amount of adrenaline comes from a packed schedule, and this can be very helpful. I've even noticed that the more I have on my plate, the more effective I am at staying on top of things. When there's not enough to do, it's easier to put things off until another time—but when "another time" doesn't exist because I've loaded my schedule, then the items get checked off faster and without fanfare. The forces of being busy bring a lot of momentum and drive. It just takes some finesse to figure out how to create a structure that is *enough* but not *too much*.

> **Bottom Line:** Being busy isn't always bad. The combination of adrenaline and having little time to waste can lead to high efficiency. We all have different thresholds for when we feel "busy" and how much activity either overwhelms or motivates us. Knowing our limits and making rational adjustments to our schedules are important aspects of self-care.

One way to think about this is that we should budget our time like we budget our money. As with our finances, we're not always good at managing our time. But some people just seem to have a knack for this, knowing what they can afford to book and when they have to say no. I'm famous for squeezing way too much in, putting undue pressure on myself, and creating a sense of urgency that could have been avoided if I were a bit more careful. I'm working to realistically estimate how much time things take and divide up my tasks accordingly.

If you tend to underestimate time, you should add an extra half hour or more to your estimates. For example, if you are planning when to arrive somewhere, you should set your departure time with some buffer room. You may believe that this will have you arrive super early—but, given your time-management difficulties, even with the extra half hour, you may end up barely making it on time. Likewise, with projects, try to account for potential hiccups to help ensure that the amount of bandwidth you've estimated aligns with what is required.

Being constantly in a hurry with a jam-packed schedule can lead to unnecessary stress. If you find yourself in that situation, you should consider scheduling downtime. A few years back, I started interjecting the word "home" on my personal calendar at least a couple of times a month, as if it were a scheduled appointment. Regardless of what invitations come up, I have committed a stretch of inviolable time to accomplishing the important task of just *being*. This gives me space to decide what I want to do and ensures that I don't have all my time gobbled up by work and errands.

Time vanishes if we aren't careful about protecting it to some degree. Doing this relies on careful planning and prioritizing what we have to commit to and then saying no to things that aren't essential. All of us have different thresholds and needs for downtime and activity. Finding the right pace and blend is an important aspect of self-care.

> **Bottom Line:** Now is your chance to start making wiser choices about how you spend your time and energy. Designating time to pursue "want to" instead of "have to" commitments is a step in the right direction. Budget your time as you would your money. Time is one of our most valuable assets.

The Big O, Human Touch, and Healing Therapies

Sex

It's inevitable. Whenever I give a workshop on RESET and ask the question "What helps you reset?" I inevitably get a nervous chuckle followed by "Sex!"—followed by some more laughs from the audience. I think they are surprised when I enthusiastically agree with their take on sex being a tremendous help when it comes to resetting.

Orgasm can indeed be a major reset, releasing tension, reducing stress, and bolstering our brain and body chemistries. Lots of people say that sex is one of the few things that helps them relax and find a calmer state. People who enjoy regular orgasms benefit from the increased blood flow it brings, and studies affirm that climaxing helps contribute to well-being.

There's more good news about orgasm. It also plays a significant role in connection. From the relational side of things, orgasm helps generate oxytocin, a powerful component of our chemistries that promotes bonding and affection.

When a person or relationship is in distress, it's not uncommon that sex comes to a halt. Our sex drives are often impacted by how stressed and/or tired we find ourselves. Many couples have come to me for therapy after very long stretches of celibacy. Sex is often the first thing that gets crossed off the list when life's tensions take over and tempers flare. Over time, this can wreak havoc. Icy bitterness and resentment, which are difficult to chisel through, can set in.

Touch

Orgasms aren't the only powerful force when it comes to touch and connection. Just ask Jackie Samuel, founder and owner of The Snuggery, who has drawn a lot of attention for selling cuddles. Samuel drew national attention when she opened her business, the first of its kind, to provide nonsexual touch for a fee. Physical affection and touch lead to lower cortisol, higher endorphins, and lower blood pressure. Even hugs are great sources of comfort. While her idea may raise eyebrows, it affirms that people benefit greatly by human touch as a means of lowering stress. When we're missing having regular touch, we can experience a tremendous void, resulting in higher stress and anxiety levels.

Many healing therapies are also built upon this premise. Reiki, massage, reflexology, and craniosacral therapy are just a few that have become increasingly sought after. There is great power in human touch.

I discovered this soon after I took on a full-time faculty position. My neck and head felt the effects of the new pressures it brought, and a dear friend suggested that I reach out to a local practitioner who was known for her craniosacral treatments. Twice a month, I enjoy a treatment, where my system is adjusted and recalibrated. I notice more energy, better sleep, and improved focus, and my neck muscles are no longer tied in knots. Talk about a reset!

Term	Definition	CONSIDER THIS
Craniosacral therapy (CST)	A gentle, hands-on approach that helps release tensions in the body.	Our limbic systems respond well to recalibration. We can sometimes have blockages that interfere with our well-being.

Acupuncture

Another standby favorite that I swear by is acupuncture. Traditional Chinese medicine has long known the power of balancing the flow of our energy, known as *qi* (pronounced "chi") in our bodies. Western medicine describes acupuncture as a way to stimulate nerves, muscles, and connective tissue, which perks up our bodies' natural painkillers and increases blood flow.

We might get creeped out when we think of needles and don't immediately associate them with relaxation. Thankfully, acupuncture isn't the least bit painful. I discovered acupuncture while writing my dissertation. My apprehension was erased after the first few minutes, when I fell into a peaceful sleep, followed by a long-lasting euphoric feeling. Sounds good, doesn't it?

At the time, my system was on overload; acupuncture helped bring my body and mind back into balance. I honestly don't think I would have made it to the finish line of my doctoral work without the support of my practitioner. His intervention brought me a great deal of stress relief and helped me feel better instantly. Getting regular treatments increased my endurance and helped equip me to harness the energy from the stress I was under and translate it into something more productive—like completing my dissertation!

In fact, my son, Ryan, who is a bit squeamish when it comes to such matters, is always willing to go for an appointment because he knows how good it will make him feel afterward. If he can do it, so can you!

Term	Definition	CONSIDER THIS
Acupuncture	One of the oldest healing practices in the world, it involves stimulation of various points in our bodies to help bolster health and well-being.	The pins used are hair thin and do not hurt. Acupuncture is known to support a wide range of health needs and is helpful in treating many emotional and physical health symptoms.

Injury and illness

Our physical health and our emotional health are intricately intertwined. Many of us battle chronic health conditions like fibromyalgia, multiple sclerosis, rheumatoid arthritis, and other autoimmune conditions. When dealing with the complexity of such illnesses, energizing becomes difficult but all the more important. This is where tailoring comes in: to evaluate what is possible and construct a reasonable plan.

Likewise, if you've ever had shoulder, back, neck, knee, or other serious injuries, you know that it's extremely difficult to muster up the willpower to find consistent routines to energize your system. Yet these types of injuries require extra resilience that can be bolstered even through deep breathing or low-impact workouts. It's essential to identify the appropriate course of action based on personal circumstances.

Many health syndromes and situations can do a number on our minds and bodies. Illness and injuries often go hand in hand with depression and anxiety. Even though it's hard to maintain consistency due to pain or fluctuations in strength, it's important to take it one day at a time, revise your plan as needed, and find things that you can do to help you reset and energize. When we're discouraged, it's not easy to imagine possibilities of positive change, but even small steps can make a big difference in our emotional health and total well-being.

If you are unconvinced and feeling unmotivated, start with something that may be surprising. Try yawning a few times with full gusto. Studies suggest that, in addition to the oxygen surge this creates, yawning positively impacts our frontal lobe, helping us to destress. (One favor: put your book down first so the unsuspecting won't think it's a reflection of what you are reading!)

> **BOTTOM LINE:** It's essential to make energizing choices according to your own preferences. Because of our different aptitudes, running and kale salads may not be everyone's first choices. You might be in a phase of life when you aren't able to get a lot of sleep, sex, or touch. As you'll see, many things are important elements in our wellness routines. Figure out which aspects are possible, and make them part of your regular self-care.

DISSECT AND REFLECT:

Am I devoting enough attention toward energizing?

As you think about the following quote, what changes do you plan to make in your existing routines?

> Movement is a medicine for creating change in a person's physical, emotional, and mental states.
> —Carol Welch

Chapter 9 in a Nutshell
Energize

1. **Intro**
   - The second principle of RESET is Energize.
   - Energizing is multifaceted; a healthy blend of activity is at the core of self-care.
   - Sallie, Jana, and Fatima all instituted changes to help them energize.
   - Energizing includes movement, diet, rest/relaxation, and touch.

2. **Move it!**
   - If the president and First Lady have time to exercise, so do we.
   - The costs of exercising are lower than not doing so.
   - Picking activities we enjoy makes us more inclined to follow through.
   - It's important to factor in age, aptitude, and abilities.
   - You don't have to be the "Biggest Loser" to win.
   - Measuring progress goes a long way.
   - Dress the part: the right attire can go a long way in fostering the right mind-set, keeping us ready to jump into the chase.

3. **You are what you eat**
   - 24-7 + McDonald's = epic health disaster.
   - Going bananas is better than going bonkers from too much salt, fat, carbs, and sugar.
   - Listen to your gut, also known as the "second brain."

4. **R³: Rest, relax, reflect**
   - Constantly burning the candle at both ends can lead to overload.

- Healthy schedules make room for transitions, reflection, play, and sleep.
- Being busy isn't necessarily bad.
- Creating a time budget helps ensure enough room to RESET.

5. **The Big O, human touch, and healing therapies**
   - Yes, sex is a RESET!
   - Snuggle up!
   - Craniosacral therapy, acupuncture, Reiki, and massage are some of the best hands-on treatments for mind and body recalibration.
   - Our mental health and physical health are intimately intertwined.

6. **Injuries and illness**
   - Devise the best plan for you, taking into account not only your schedule but also any injuries or illnesses you may have.

10

SOOTHE

Nothing is chaotic as it seems. Nothing is worth your health.
Nothing is worth poisoning yourself in anxiety, stress, and fear.
—Steve Maraboli

ESSENTIAL QUESTION: What measures do you
take to soothe your stress?

Decompress your stress

When it comes to making the most of our stress, there's a lot of
attention on the mind, body, and spirit, but our senses are often
overlooked as powerful tools for restoration. Take Barry Parker, for
example, who discovered the power of soothing to counteract how
tightly he was wound. After two and a half hours in traffic, his head,
neck, and shoulders ached. He was tired, hungry, and discombobulated.
Arriving home, he wanted nothing more than to collapse on the couch
with a giant pizza and mug of his favorite brew. Knowing he'd feel
even worse, he opted for some soup and a few laps around the block.
He later curled up with a good book and turned some of his favorite
jazz on, which always seemed to have a calming effect.

This choice wasn't easy, but Barry had learned that he needed to do something calming after a long battle with traffic. In addition to the in-the-moment strategies he employed, he also made sure that he was going for regular massages, getting his runs in, and carving out time for the favorite people in his life.

For all of us, when under any form of stress, we instinctively try to soothe ourselves. We frantically search for remedies to help us get back to some sort of homeostasis. We select either adaptive or maladaptive ways of carrying this out, resulting in either extra insulation from stress or magnification of what we are enduring. In other words, we either improve our situation or make matters worse.

The third principle of RESET is Soothe

Soothing is at the front and center of self-care, with our aesthetic and sensory meters driving our behavior.

Our senses tell us a lot about our thresholds. Soothing is directly related to our senses—taste, smell, sight, touch, hearing—and our gut instincts. Our senses are powerful. They help to signal and relieve stress. Consider the impact of a hot bath, beautiful sunset, or fragrant cup of coffee. Consider the feeling you get after a good laugh with a friend. These sensations help counteract the constant bombardment our senses endure from the many demands and experiences of life. We can easily get overstimulated by what we're taking in, causing our circuits to overload, and often, causing anxiety.

This is a well-known fact to advertisers. Remember the Calgon "Take Me Away" commercial? So many products are pitched to appeal to our need to relax. Billions of dollars are spent annually on products and prescriptions that promise to curb our stress and soothe us in one form or another. Scented candles, lotions, captivating paint colors, fleece blankets, turbo vitamins, herbal teas, ice-cold beer, fine wines, and chocolates are among the many things thrust at us to create a more soothing environment and mental state.

Besides what we ingest, it can be extremely helpful to create an environment that we find both soothing and inspiring. Some people notice that moving furniture or decorations around or tidying up a cluttered room can make a huge difference in their mental state. When our environments are too overstimulating or too lacking in aesthetic appeal, it may increase our stress.

Marla Cilley knows this. Self-proclaimed as the "FlyLady,"[59] she has drawn a huge audience with her de-cluttering tips, broken down into manageable pieces. Her cultish following affirms that many of us need structure and guidance around how to create more soothing environments. When spaces are cluttered, this can contribute to stress, and many find it refreshing to do some revamping to make room for calm.

> **Bottom Line:** There's something to be said about how we set up and maintain our space. Our environments can be overstimulating or soothing. Sometimes it's necessary to call in the experts and enlist a cleaner/ organizer to help.

While often helpful, even appealing environments can fall short when it comes to stress relief. The need to soothe can sometimes trump discretion—and the traps of drinking too much, drug use, or overeating in order to "soothe" ourselves can diminish our self-care efforts. Even when we have the best intentions, our need to soothe ourselves can lead to doing so in nonadaptive ways. This is a reality indicated by the extreme addiction rates seen in the United States and in many other countries around the world.

Eat, drink, text, and be unhealthy

We have made a pastime of consuming heaping amounts of screen time, fast food, and booze, among other things. Our brains light up with dopamine, and our systems get juiced with adrenaline when we soothe with such measures, leaving us coming back for more but

---

[59]   See http://www.FlyLady.net/ to learn more.

not fully nourished or satisfied—in fact, often badly served by such attempts at self-soothing.

We crave information, and our phones and tablets have become like appendages. Many jobs demand high screen time, and when we leave work, we're still constantly texting, tweeting, snap chatting, Instagramming, and posting on our favorite social media sites. Many of us struggle with resisting the urge to repeatedly check for the latest text, e-mail, posting, or newsflash. There is both a pressure to keep up and a measure of stimulation and soothing that comes with it all.

Some of us fall into the trap of watching and listening to news incessantly. We forget that most media outlets deliberately draw attention to negative stories to bolster ratings. Our desire to stay up-to-date can lead us to be unnecessarily worked up rather than comforted.

Advertisers are able to appeal to one of our strongest instincts—our appetite for food. Food addiction and obesity are becoming hallmark characteristics of the American population. In fact, in the United States, obesity is second only to tobacco as a cause of preventable deaths. We can easily fall into the trap of soothing ourselves from stress with food. This has obviously wreaked havoc on more than our waistlines. Diabetes, high blood pressure, heart disease, and cancer are all associated with obesity.

This isn't a moral failing, per se. Our brains are bombarded with messages of distress and distraction, knocking us off-center. The brain realizes that "something is wrong" and wants relief. We get knots in our neck, tension headaches, pounding hearts. We feel depleted, exhausted, and frazzled. We crave sugar, caffeine, and carbs. We look for something to numb the powerful and intense feelings of pain that stress can bring.

Prescription and illicit drug abuse and rates of alcoholism are indicators of the desperation many of us endure. Drug and alcohol abuse have long been dubbed "self-medication." We want to escape from the sensations our brains and bodies experience in the throes of distress. We may find ourselves in such a wound-up state that we'd rather be numb than have to face this utter sensory and emotional overload. When we're wound up or worn out, our defenses go down, and we sometimes become less discerning about our choices about how to soothe ourselves. Many people come to therapy and soon realize that their excess drinking relates to their trouble managing stress.

Soothe it or lose it

Soothing helps our minds and bodies. From putting on our favorite broken-in pair of sweatpants to taking a big whiff of ocean air to really tasting a morning cup of coffee, soothing matters. Our brains like getting the message that "things are okay." When we foster a sense of comfort, this influences our stress. When we stay present with the positive sensations long enough to really enjoy them, it can do a world of good. These things can help turn the power of stress into positive momentum.

Since soothing is instinctual, we must ensure that we select modes of soothing that help. We can to begin paying better attention to the way we take things in. If we're rushing through things or constantly in fifth gear, our senses may be overloaded and tip us in the direction of anxiety. Many of us end up clenching our jaws, holding our breath, wolfing down our food, and gulping our tea—and forget to slow down and experience these positive sensations.

Our senses help us process a great deal of information directly tied to our inner state and overall well-being. They help alert us to trouble (the smell of smoke, the sight of someone's grimace, the sound of thunder). They also help us relax and enjoy an experience (the smell of a baby, the taste of our favorite dish, the feeling of an embrace). But when our adrenaline is constantly pumping, our bodies and brains receive messages that seem to indicate that something is wrong. Choosing to send a different message to them can help counteract this.

Making deliberate choices around soothing allows us to take the momentum created by stress and translate it into something more positive and productive.

> **Bottom Line:** Adaptive soothing has to do with identifying things that may not be so good for the long-term bottom line: drinking, too much TV, inactivity. It means noticing when we're rushing through something without taking in the positive sensations generated from the sights, sounds, and smells around us. Likewise, if something in our senses triggers or bothers us, it's good to see if we can remove, reduce, or cope with it—or if we can send a different, positive message to our senses instead.

Life is one giant sensory experience

So how can we send the message to our brain that everything is going to be okay? How can we RESET along these lines? I often ask people what works for them. Some of the answers I've gotten, along with my own tried and true tricks, include the following:[60]

- letting it out with a good cry
- having a hearty belly laugh
- working up an invigorating sweat
- experiencing a powerful orgasm
- giving/receiving a great big bear hug
- spending time in prayer, meditation, and solitude
- taking a deep, cleansing breath
- engaging in a creative art project
- singing, dancing, and playing music
- sipping a steaming mug of tea or coffee
- curling up with a good book
- taking yoga classes

---

[60] You can find more under the "Recommendation for Further Growth" section at the back of this book.

- soaking in hot Epsom salt baths[61]
- playing and cuddling with pets
- spending time with children

Are these on your list of regular experiences? If not, what can you add to help with soothing?

BOTTOM LINE: Are you feeling hot, hot, hot? Temperature influences our soothing. Consider the difference between a hot or cold shower, drink, or day. For each, what do you prefer? Knowing that about yourself, do you take time to absorb this aspect of sensation?

In lots of ways, life is one giant sensory experience. Our sight, hearing, touch, taste, and sense of smell play a large role in our emotional states. By paying attention to what's around us, we can feel more grounded and enjoy ourselves. Our senses are powerful components of resetting. This is an amazing facet of our humanness. By taking advantage of our senses and making the most of our surroundings, we can directly reduce the toll of stress on our minds and bodies.

BOTTOM LINE: Soothing involves careful attention to the way we take things in and how this, in turn, impacts our well-being.

---

[61]   This is an old standby from way back that has become trendy again! My Grandma Jennie, who lived to be 103, was famous for her old-timer remedies that magically worked for a range of ailments. Vicks VapoRub for coughs, aloe for skin irritations, and Epsom salt for aches were among the many interventions she swore by. The Epsom salt contains magnesium, which is known to have soothing qualities. As a bonus, it's extremely helpful to muscles after long workouts/runs. Hot baths and showers give us time in seclusion to think or even belt out a tune!

Dissect and Reflect

- In what ways am I enjoying the stimuli that surround me?
- What changes would make a difference in helping me enjoy my environment better?

Chapter 10 in a Nutshell
Soothe

1. **Decompress your stress**
   - Our senses are powerful and are often overlooked when it comes to developing a self-care plan.

2. **The third principle of RESET is Soothe**
   - Soothing is at the center of self-care.
   - We soothe in either positive, adaptive ways or in a self-destructive manner.
   - Our taste, smell, sight, touch, and gut instincts alert us and impact our aesthetic preferences.

3. **Eat, drink, text, and be unhealthy**
   - American consumption is at an all-time high.
   - Information cravings can leave us chained to our screens.
   - Obesity rates are of epic proportions nationwide.
   - More than ever, we are self-medicating with drugs, alcohol, food and technology to try to soothe.

4. **Soothe it or lose it**
   - We often rush through comforting experiences and miss their positive impact.
   - Our senses provide valuable information that alerts us about what we need more or less of.
   - The nonstop demands flooding our sensory circuits can take their toll and need counteracting.

5. **Life is one giant sensory experience**
   - A good cry, laugh, sweat, orgasm, and hug can be stimulating and soothing.
   - By leveraging the power of our senses, we will find more enjoyment in our surroundings.

11

END UNPRODUCTIVE
THINKING

Whatever happens will be ... for the air speaks of
all we'll never be ... it won't trouble me.
—Glen Phillips and Toad the Wet Sprocket

ESSENTIAL QUESTION: What if we were able to reclaim
all the time spent on worrying and unproductive
thinking and use it for learning and growth?

Out with the old, in with the new

The fourth principle of RESET is END UNPRODUCTIVE THINKING. Our
minds want to work hard, and if we're not careful, we can end up
spinning our wheels without much to show for it. When we engage
in thinking that helps us make the most of our stress, it goes a long
way toward ending, or at least controlling it's potential impact. We
often need to ditch our old ways of doing things to make room for
productive pursuits that work better. Unproductive thinking can rent
all the space in our heads, leaving us with little time and energy for

more productive endeavors. They say that most of what we worry about never comes to fruition, yet it's natural to get trapped on the anxiety treadmill.

Focus on Productive Thinking

Unproductive thinking can take a variety of forms, as we've seen already. It can involve ruminating over what was said or not said, done or not done—and end up being quite toxic. Unproductive thinking involves a desire for something to be a certain way, but it often takes a wrong turn, leaving us marinating in stress and unable even to see what that desire is and what resources we have—within ourselves and in our environment—to achieve that desire.

Ending unproductive thinking is directly linked to the Realize step of RESET. Our peak unproductive times are often when we are in "first appraisal" mode, before we've had time to sort things out and understand what is triggering our mental avalanche. When we engage in the Realize step, we make way for productive thinking; doing so helps stop unproductive thinking and greatly contributes momentum toward our self-care.

Productive thinking can bring renewed excitement over our goals and dreams. It gives us room to be creative and to entertain new possibilities for ourselves. There are many versions of productive thinking to draw upon. Productive thinking involves learning, problem solving, goal setting, anchoring down positive memories, remembering ways we've been resilient, dreaming, visualizing events or scenarios in positive ways, and rehearsing success in upcoming events. When we engage in productive thinking, we directly reinforce positive thoughts and emotions and undermine negative ones. This makes room for more productive endeavors, contributing toward our growth and development.

Learn, baby, learn!

Education is powerful. Knowledge helps us to decipher various aspects of life and promotes deeper understanding. Even seemingly insignificant pieces of information can make a huge difference in how we see the world and engage in it. When we're pursuing learning, we have less time to involve ourselves in unproductive thinking. Along with faith and relationships, education has been a transformational force in my life. It has helped me develop insight and perspective.

There's so much to learn about human nature. From small nuggets of insight about self-care to complex theories, endless educational opportunities can directly shape our lives. Some of us are interested in getting a formal education by taking courses or seeking advanced degrees. Others may just want to have a better understanding of self or a particular topic and would benefit from the many blogs and articles available online.

I've seen the power of information sharing throughout my career as a clinical social worker. Therapy is educational. There's so much to learn about human behavior and functioning. When we understand communication and relationship principles, it improves the quality of our lives. Even simple strategies can go a long way. Whether learning about how personalities influence behavior or how our strengths and weaknesses are often intricately related, we benefit immensely from a deeper understanding of known strategies and skills for living to our fullest potential.

> **Bottom Line:** If we foster a deeper understanding of what's healthy and what's not, it can generate new momentum to follow through with thoughts and activities that are positive and productive.

Unfortunately, we sometimes waste time on mindless activities that don't do very much good for our personal and intellectual development. Many traps and distractions can suck away our time. Instead, we should commit ourselves to being what we call in education "lifelong learners." Expanding our knowledge can bolster our cognitive skills, self-confidence, and happiness. In order to do this, we can make room for new activities to increase our intellectual finesse. Here are some terrific ways to develop your skills and build upon what you're already doing:

- **EdX:** Powerhouse universities MIT, Harvard, Berkeley, and the University of Texas have joined forces in a groundbreaking way to offer free courses on a wide range of topics. See https:// www.edx.org/ to begin your journey. Anyone can take them!
- **TED Talks:** Known as "riveting talks by remarkable people, free to the world," thousands of speakers will support your development and RESET goals. One of my favorite talks is "How to Make Stress Your Friend," by Kelly McGonical. Go to http:// www.ted.com/ to select from a wide range of talks that will stay with you long after you watch them.
- **Community resources:** Virtually every community has some sort of learning network to tap into. Scour your local websites, newspapers, and bulletin boards for leads.
- **Toastmasters International:** Sharpen your communication and people skills in a supportive and structured way. This has proven to be a wonderful resource that has stood the test of time. Learn more at http://www.toastmasters.org/.
- **Professional organizations:** Most occupations have professional associations, with some offering web resources, journal articles, and conferences. Joining up with people in

your profession is a great way to connect and grow. There are a nearly endless number of different opportunities that you may enjoy within your discipline or related areas. Try Google for ideas.

- **Your local library:** Never underestimate the power of reading. Librarians may be stereotypically pegged as quirky, but they are a wealth of information. Intellectual stimulation is helpful for our emotional bottom line. When we engage in learning and other similar endeavors, it is time well spent. While there are a myriad of wonderful books out there, you may also want to read articles and short pieces that offer information and compelling writing. Along these lines, documentaries and biographies are outstanding ways to become inspired through personal stories of resilience and perseverance.

> **BOTTOM LINE:** When we're engaged in stimulating activity, there's less chance of being taken over by the unhelpful mental chatter that often wants to dominate our thinking.

Talk to Yourself!

It's so easy to fall into the trap of getting stressed about being stressed and beating ourselves up for our perceived shortcomings. Remembering that stress isn't all bad is a lesson that sometimes has trouble sticking. We need to become our own coaches to constantly reinforce the idea that struggle and suffering can build our character, develop our empathy, and even influence our behavior in a positive way (someone in a dysfunctional home breaking the cycle; person with addiction issues that becomes a therapist). Because life can be so challenging, ongoing coaching helps keep our thinking on the productive side of things. This, in essence, requires our active, ongoing participation in talking to ourselves!

Negative thoughts are born out of stress, and it takes work to delete them and refocus our energies. It's a lot easier to beat ourselves up when something goes wrong instead of slowing down and thoughtfully piecing things together. As we learned in chapter 4, our tendencies to sprint, skip, and tumble are strong. It takes a measure of strength and resolve to resist the urge to have an "I hate myself and the world" heyday.

The way we think affects virtually every area of our lives. The views we adopt profoundly influence the way we approach challenges, make meaning of ourselves (and others), and navigate the many challenges inherent in being human. We need to be deliberate about how we think and intentional about redirecting our thoughts when they become too rigid or toxic. This is the cornerstone of good therapy and, in essence, good living.

> **BOTTOM LINE:** Life's whoppers bait us into negative thinking patterns. It takes a measure of awareness and planning to redirect our thinking, especially when we are facing trials of all shapes and sizes.

One helpful coaching tool is developing a mantra, which is a slogan to be repeated often that affirms a positive thought or feeling state. Mantras are used on sports fields, in twelve-step communities, in classrooms, and in companies to keep focus and inspiration at the forefront. We can use them ourselves for the same purpose and to keep our RESET momentum ramped up.

Term	Definition	CONSIDER THIS
Mantra	Slogan that affirms a "can-do" attitude and helps us refocus negative thinking toward our desired goals and feeling states.	Mantras can be simple or complex, but picking something that is memorable and repeating it often is key.

Mantra examples:

- "I can do it."
- "It's all good."
- "One day at a time."
- "Stick to it."
- "Keep moving."
- "This too shall pass."
- "Live and let live."
- "Keep calm and carry on."

Quotes are a great resource when developing a mantra. You can find them in scripture, from inspirational people, and all over the Internet. Quotes give us a focal point and incentivize us to remember the big picture. These succinct reminders keep us company on our journey.

I've known people who have based their mantra on this famous quote by Chuck Swindoll:

> The longer I live, the more I realize the impact of attitude on life. Attitude, to me, is more important than facts. It is more important than the past, than education, than money, than circumstances, than failures, than successes, than what other people think or say or do. It is more important than appearance, giftedness, or skill. It will make or break a company ... a church ... a home. The remarkable thing is we have a choice every day regarding the attitude we will embrace for that day. We cannot change our past ... we cannot change the fact that people will act in a certain way. We cannot change the inevitable. The only thing we can do is play on the one string we have, and that is our attitude ... I am convinced that life is 10 percent what happens to me and 90 percent how I react to it. And so it is with you ... we are in charge of our attitudes.

While it may be hard to memorize such a lengthy quote, a mantra can be developed from it to help keep it in the forefront of your mind. Consider using a shortened version like "attitude matters," "keep it in check," or "make or break it!" You can pick your own quote that resonates with you and carve out a mantra that will support self-coaching efforts. When we coach and talk to ourselves in positive, productive ways, it goes a long way. It means that we're working to make sense of things in a way that calls on the many skills and resources within our reach.

Pick a Mantra to Promote Productive Thinking

Sometimes mantras are gimmicky and seem trite. When this is the case, they are unlikely to take us the distance. One of my all-time favorite *Saturday Night Live* skits was Al Franken's depiction of Stuart Smalley, the "therapist who is a member of several twelve-step groups but not actually licensed" (or at all credible). In the skit, there's no shortage of syrupy "positive affirmations," like "I'm good enough, I'm smart enough, and doggonit, people like me!" In real life, all that corniness just doesn't cut it. Stuart Smalley is a hilarious reminder that we need to stay concrete, with practical, positive ideas that avoid stereotypical, touchy-feely tones.

> **Bottom Line:** Be positive, but don't pull a Stuart Smalley! Keep your self-talk and affirmations snappy and real!

Keeping our sense of humor helps us keep perspective. Even when something seems catastrophic at the moment, it can turn into an amusing story later. When we can laugh at our inconsistencies and calamities, it helps us avoid getting mired in unproductive thinking. Our bloopers may not seem funny at first, but if we can find amusement in our own—and others'—idiosyncrasies and behavior, we can regain crucial balance in how we perceive the world and our journey through it.

> **BOTTOM LINE:** Pick a mantra that resonates with you. Go with your instincts, and find a quote or line that motivates you. Picture yourself as your own coach, and keep reinforcing the message. Over time, it will stick. Keep your sense of humor—you'll likely need it.

Sometimes we take ourselves too seriously, sabotaging our coaching efforts. Other times, we don't take seriously enough how much time and energy we should devote to learning and growth. Ending both types of thinking is vital. When we evaluate our tendencies, we are better equipped to reset ourselves from the ill effects of unproductive thinking.

Friends can help us find humor and shake things off faster. As we'll see in the next chapter, we need to enlist the support of people in our lives to help us with our coaching endeavors.

DISSECT AND REFLECT

- How much time do you spend embroiled in unproductive thinking? What types of themes do you notice?
- Which aspects of your thought process seem most productive?
- What is your mantra? What additional sayings and quotes can you add in your repertoire for maximum impact?

Chapter 11 in a Nutshell
End Unproductive Thinking

1. **Out with the old, in with the new**
   - When unproductive thinking occupies too much space in our heads, we have less capacity for productive endeavors.
   - Unproductive thinking sabotages rational thinking and is often at its peak when we're in the primary appraisal stage.

2. **The fourth principle of RESET is END UNPRODUCTIVE THINKING**
   - The Realize step in RESET helps facilitate productive thinking.
   - Productive thinking helps us problem solve, set goals, practice positive visualization, and anchor down positive thoughts and emotions.

3. **Learn, baby, learn!**
   - When we stimulate our minds, we generate energy and growth that helps fight against waves of unproductive thinking.
   - Education—whether about self-care or otherwise—helps boost our RESET capacity.
   - Make room for EdX, Ted Talks, and your local librarian!

4. **Talk to yourself!**
   - Be your own coach.
   - It's a constant effort to redirect our thinking.
   - Mantras help anchor down our resolve and keep a fresh sense of hope and purpose.
   - Keep it real: Stuart Smalley–type gimmicks don't cut it, but humor can bring great relief!

12

TALK IT OUT

Think of your head as an unsafe
neighborhood; don't go there alone.
—Augusten Burroughs

ESSENTIAL QUESTION: Is what you're saying
and are the people you're sharing it with helping
you reach your goals?

The fifth principle of RESET is TALK IT OUT

Kramer, Jerry Seinfeld's infamous neighbor, is worked up. He
frantically grabs Seinfeld, his best friend, demanding his attention
and help. He then proceeds to fire off a long list of things bothering
him, barely coming up for air, in true Kramer fashion. Seinfeld is
attentive, nodding and clearly engaged, but can't get a word in
edgewise. When Kramer stops, he then proceeds to thank Jerry for
his great wisdom and advice. Seinfeld smiles and shakes his head at
his neighbor's shenanigans, knowing that "all he did" was listen.

The *Seinfeld* show had a knack for hitting the nail on the head when
it came to presenting human behavior. We laugh because we relate
to the idiosyncrasies of life as depicted through various screwball

characters in the show. We've seen this scene play out in countless movies, TV shows, and in our own relationships. When people stop to listen, it means a lot. A good debriefing is refreshing, and it is often surprising how much it can actually help. We benefit greatly from getting "things off our chest" as we try to put things into perspective. Holding stress in is detrimental to our health, well-being, and, of course, our RESET potential.

Sometimes we even need to vent about "small" things, letting our thoughts be heard. Something powerful occurs when we verbalize what we are thinking, helping us to process and develop perspective in a different way than when we're mentally stewing over our problems. Talking helps us problem solve in ways that just thinking by itself cannot do.

Therapy exists for this reason. Thinking out loud not only allows a therapist to guide us but also helps us develop new insights that have the power to disrupt negative thought and behavior patterns. It helps us to reframe and reaffirm our motivation for change and improvement. Moreover, when we feel listened to, we feel greatly relieved and validated.

However, "talking traps" can make our venting less productive. As with unproductive thinking, unproductive talking traps are easiest to fall into immediately after an unsettling event or interaction first happens. We often are spurred on by anxiety or too much adrenaline in these moments. Our brains may be saturated or overwhelmed, and we desperately need to process. As we've seen, talking is important! However, we may need to be sure that we are not compounding our problems and affecting those in our firing range. Unproductive talking can consist of:

- **Repetition:** Saying the same things over and over
- **Little substance:** Not much meat to what is being shared
- **High frustration:** Constant complaining about self or others; trouble letting go

> **Bottom Line:** Eleanor Roosevelt was known for her golden nuggets of wisdom, including "Great minds discuss ideas, average minds discuss events, and small minds discuss people." Frustration is inevitable within our relationships, but spending too much time complaining interferes with enjoying more substantive conversations and contemplations.

Aimless venting about every person or problem bothering us sometimes leads to more misery and hinders our capacity to slow down and listen. Lots of times, we become hypertalkative when we are anxious or overstimulated. It takes time and maturity to reduce the verbal gymnastics we may be engaging in. I remember offering my husband, Scott, the daily play-by-play of my interactions when we were first married and I was training as a clinician. Over time, I've learned to cope in new ways, so that verbalizing the nitty-gritty of my experience isn't the only way to let some steam off. In other words, I don't have to share every thought, feeling, and response I've had throughout the course of a day. Instead, I can let go of things without getting as worked up as I once did. This gives us more time to talk about other important matters, and I am quite sure Scott is grateful for the modifications I have made over time!

Watch out for Talking Traps!

Make the connection

Healthy relationships help us stay healthy. Finding people who not only listen well but will also offer honest, thoughtful feedback is essential. Another aspect of Talk it out is identifying healthy people to trust and rely upon. Choosing what we say and who we say it to is a huge component of maintaining momentum with self-care.

Part of RESET involves evaluating your current support system. Colleagues, friends, and family can be invaluable resources, and unfortunately, they can also bring out the worst in us. We have to be on the lookout to find trusted confidants who truly care about our best interests, without a competing agenda or ulterior motives.

It's worth assessing which relationships tend to bring you joy and which ones drag you down. Maybe people in your life are constantly giving you their version of the play-by-play, and it's wearing you out. Or you may notice that your efforts toward improvement are met with negative responses or disinterest. You may have to steer people in a different direction by asking them for more or less of something they are doing.

Communicating our needs has to do with boundaries. Boundaries help us define what we can tolerate—and what we cannot. They help us express what we expect from ourselves and others. Boundaries help us avoid being too lenient with others and not expecting enough, and they also involve letting our guards down enough to trust others and rely on someone when we need them. This is harder than it may seem.

Term	Definition	Consider This
Boundaries	Defining lines of what we consider acceptable or permissible within social interactions and relationships.	Boundaries are a way to help maintain healthy relationships with those in your life; if they are too thin, we permit people to walk all over us; if they are too thick, we have walls up and won't "let people in."

Building a support network involves looking for people who seem balanced, positive, and wise. Healthy people often gravitate toward one another since they have a level of confidence and security that makes them more prone to listen, not judge, and to offer helpful and honest feedback. If you spend time with others who are not committed to maintaining a healthy perspective, it can hamper your self-care momentum.

If your loved ones can't be persuaded to help support your growth and happiness, you may decide that you need to set new boundaries with them or to expand your network to include new and interesting people who can do this. I'm not suggesting crossing lots of people off your list, but it is worth examining how your relationships are affecting you and what fits best with your goals for staying positive. The adage "misery loves company" is, unfortunately, often accurate about human nature.

"Co-rumination," a term coined by Dr. Amanda Rose, an associate professor of psychology at the University of Missouri–Columbia, describes the process by which friends focus on sharing thoughts and self-perceptions with each other to the exclusion of other activities—culminating in what has been described as a "contagious effect" of pessimistic thinking among friends or social groups. Talk about misery. It's easy to get sucked into these habits, wasting time and sidetracking you from your RESET goals.

Patti's story

When Patti came to me for therapy, we immediately began talking about her support system, or, to be more accurate, her lack of one. Her best friend, Jenna, was what she called a "chronic complainer," who sent a daily barrage of Facebook messages and texts that were nothing short of a major pity party. Patti felt conflicted since they had been friends for years, through thick and thin, yet Jenna's negativity was getting out of hand. Patti had a few other friends, but for the most part, she spent the majority of her time hanging out with Jenna.

Over time, Patti and I spoke about her relational needs. She started to realize how much she loved to laugh and wanted to be around what she called "fun and funny" people. This insight led her to join up with a local group she found online who met every other Friday to play games.[62] Patti ended up loving the types of people she met, which lifted her spirits dramatically.

Bottom Line: Positive, authentic friends and colleagues can give us a huge lift. They're worth searching for, and when you find them, don't let them go. Relationships take time and effort and are worth investing in.

Building off her initial success, Patti also realized that there were some great people at work, and she asked her colleague Kara to start walking at lunch. These lunch walks were electrifying for Patti, since over time they started to talk about goals and shared ideas about favorite books, life strategies, and more.

Eventually, Patti decided that it was time to gently inform Jenna that her excessive negativity was bothersome. She started to set boundaries on how much she allowed

---

[62] Under "Recommendations for Further Growth," check out "Meet Up," an online place to connect with others around your favorite activities. While there are dating options available, many don't involve romance, and they offer fun group events.

Jenna to rant and worked to redirect her to look at the big picture and focus on something more positive. Patti started talking in an upbeat way, and while Jenna still remained a bit stuck, she started following suit. While Patti still kept ties to Jenna, she diversified her range of friends, which brought her a lot of joy and helped bolster her confidence and sense of well-being.

Patti's original problem is not uncommon. People in all stages of life experience trouble finding quality relationships. It can be difficult to find others who are on the same wavelength and willing to carry their weight in the relationship. Sometimes, people take more than they can give and are unable to reciprocate acts of kindness and active listening. Part of self-care involves evaluating mutuality in our relationships. You will unlikely find a fifty-fifty split in your relationships, but if you notice that most of your relationships are lopsided, you may need to make some changes.

Term	Definition	CONSIDER THIS
Mutuality	Reciprocal respect and level of engagement invested in a relationship.	It's important in relationships that both parties are willing to support one another; having too many one-sided relationships can be detrimental.

BOTTOM LINE: With some friends, we have high degrees of mutuality, and with others, we are in a supporting role. This isn't necessarily bad; it's just important that as a whole your relationships do not lean too heavily to one side or another (giving or taking). If our relationships are extremely disproportionate, we may miss out on something we need or can give in other relationships.

Patti offers a good example of the benefits of assessing our relationships. Sometimes when we're in the strong role, the person relying on us has a hard time realizing that we have needs too. When someone we care about is going through difficulty, we often avoid speaking about our own concerns, feeling that they shouldn't be brought up in the face of something dramatically worse. Over time, we can lose the courage to ask for support for what are facing. This is damaging on both ends. The person in the strong role may feel disappointed and that their needs don't matter. The person in the more dependent role may not feel needed or may feel that listening to the "strong" person's concerns would give them a break from their own worries.

Relationships can surely leave us dissatisfied. People are not perfect, and sometimes the longer we know someone, the more flaws come through. Still, most of us yearn for intimate, authentic relationships where we can be known for who we are and know others in the same way. Feeling comfortable being ourselves is a major contributing factor toward relationship success and happiness.

There are many paradoxes in relationships. It takes effort and rebound and resolve to trust again. Still, realizing who we are in the context of our relationships can be powerful. It can take a few tries before we get to the point of authentic relationships, but it is worth the effort.

> **Bottom Line:** It's rare that one person will fulfill our relationship needs, but participating in a range of relationships with varying levels of mutuality can help. We have to learn to speak up and ask for what we need and be willing to give, as well.

Build a strong network

In my clinical practice, I have had the privilege of working with a wide range of age groups. I've been surprised at how many young people are affected by loneliness, experiencing tremendous difficulty finding and keeping healthy relationships.

It's not unexpected that the elderly often deal with social isolation. Often, their significant others and peers have passed away, and as they age, they have greater trouble getting out and about. But the fact that many young people are lonely seems like a contradiction in today's hyperconnected world. While social networking sites, texting, and so on provide us with the means to connect to one another more than ever before, there's a downside: it seems that when we're unplugged, we tend to be more lonely and distant from one another. Dr. Sherry Turkle is one of many social psychologists who worry that being constantly plugged in can strain our personal relationships.[63]

The advent of new technologies and social media have brought amazing innovation, but not without a price. There is a pressure to "keep up" and an inability to fully escape from work or catch a moment of solitude. The checklist of demands has grown so long that quality time is hard to find. Even with multiple means of connecting, such research as Dr. Turkle's shows that people feel more disconnected than ever. Do your own human behavior experiment and go out to eat on a Friday night. Look around and notice the number of people who are more involved with interacting on their devices than they are with each other. It's become commonplace, but to me, is still a bit shocking and disheartening.

> **BOTTOM LINE:** When we build relationships with others, we become more connected and content. We face demands and distractions that compete for our time and attention. It takes awareness and effort to ensure that we are connecting with others in meaningful ways.

I've learned that having a diverse range of relationships can be both enjoyable and helpful. While we sometimes gravitate toward

---

[63]   Dr. Turkle's book, *Alone Together,* helps illuminate the impact of screen time on human interactions.

people who are like us, are the same age or in the same stage of life, or tell us what we want to hear, it's often people who are different from us who can offer us rich relational experiences. I have friends from many places and from various cultures and life experiences. I've always been drawn to people who are different from me and am fascinated by the wide range of perspectives they bring.

If we limit our relationships to people who look, think, or act similarly to us, we miss out. Similarly, if we gravitate toward people who are too agreeable to our viewpoints, we may lose out on opportunities to challenge our thinking and grow beyond what we know at a given moment. Having diverse relationships helps stretch our boundaries and broaden our perspectives.

The power of mentoring

Some of the best relationships I've ever been part of are ones where I am being mentored or mentoring someone else. Throughout our lives, we look to people who have gathered wisdom and insights and can share them with us. Mentoring allows for a shared process of making sense of life, and it offers support that goes a long way.

I've had some powerful mentors who have given so much. I've found mentors at school, work, in my community, and at church. Along the way, my various mentors saw potential in me and wanted to support me in reaching my goals. I have had many mentors who have shaped my path and that I am indebted to. Their investment has propelled me to offer myself to others in a similar fashion, which is so much a part of human connection.

Term	Definition	CONSIDER THIS
Mentor	A trusted advisor or counselor supporting learning goals, personal development, and growth.	A mentor can be a wonderful role model and help bring out the best in us.

While being mentored is tremendously valuable, there is also something to be said for mentoring others. We can share what we have learned, which also turns out to be a dynamic process. Having a mentee is a wonderful way to contribute toward someone else's development and also affirms our knowledge and sense of altruism. When we've received such support, it's rewarding to be able to turn around and give back.

Term	Definition	Consider This
Mentee	Often known as a "protégé"; a person who seeks a supportive, nurturing advisor to help with personal and/or professional development.	Mentoring others can be extremely rewarding; building the potential of others can bolster our confidence and enhance our satisfaction.

Bottom Line: The quote "People will forget what you said or did but not how you made them feel" is a great reminder of the value of our relationships.

Endless possibilities abound when it comes to building a strong network. The "Recommendation for Further Growth" section at the end of this book lists resources. Between connecting with new people, finding a mentor/mentee, and engaging in professional organizations, social groups, community events, and enrichment activities, many ways exist to meet new people and expand our networks in a thoughtful manner. By staying engaged and connected, we reduce the risk of isolation and discouragement. We can contribute to others' lives and also receive support. Finding dynamic people to talk to and create community with are essential components of our RESET plans.

Dissect and Reflect

- Who are my most trusted confidants?
- Are my boundaries too thick or thin?
- What relationships need some attention?
- What opportunities exist that will help me expand my support network?

Chapter 12 in a Nutshell
Talk It Out

1. **The fifth principle of RESET is TALK IT OUT**
   - Never underestimate the power of being listened to.
   - A good debriefing is refreshing.
   - Thinking out loud helps us regain perspective.
   - Talking traps like repetition, lack of substance, or putting ourselves/others down hinder progress.

2. **Make the connection**
   - Healthy relationships help us stay healthy.
   - Communicating what we need more or less of is essential.
   - Assessing our relationships and the roles we play in them helps us to set boundaries and work toward mutuality.
   - Relationships are complex and paradoxical; it takes effort to build healthy connections.

3. **Build a strong network.**
   - Diverse perspectives help us understand ourselves and the world better.
   - Find a mentor to support your learning and growth, and reach out to others in the same way.
   - Keep active in professional, community, and social groups.

PART 3

Maintaining Your Sense of Well-Being: Your RESET Plan of Action

❧ Phase 1: Evaluate: What's Working Well and What's Not? ❧

❧ Phase 2: Prioritize: Set Target Goals ❧

❧ Phase 3: Implement: Bring Your RESET Plan to Life ❧

PHASE 1

EVALUATE: WHAT'S WORKING WELL, AND WHAT'S NOT?

You don't have to see the whole staircase, just take the first step.
—Dr. Martin Luther King Jr.

ESSENTIAL QUESTION: Can I *really* change?

You *can* teach an old dog new tricks

Change is not a linear process. It takes lots of trips back to the drawing board to evaluate exactly what is needed and how it can be accomplished. Bringing your RESET plan to life will require careful planning, much support, persistence, and plenty of practice. While three phases are described here, they are not so much chronological checklists as they are frameworks for you to craft your own unique plan. As we've discussed, your self-care efforts should be the right fit for *your* life circumstances—not your friends' or your partner's. Just like you, your plan will continue to evolve and progress over time.

Look for islands

When people learn that I am a therapist, they often ask, "Do you think people can actually change?" Many feel that once we are set in our ways, it's unlikely that we can break old habits. Luckily, this belief is wrong. Human progress is always possible.

Fortunately, we are all capable of change. But as we've talked about, carryover is difficult. We can want badly to reach our goals but have trouble with follow-through. This is something I have dealt with in my own life and see consistently in those I am working with.

It takes a lot of effort to stick with our goals. Starting and stopping is natural. We face inevitable pushes and pulls. In scripture, references abound to "battles of the flesh." Indeed, an epic tension often exists between what we know we should do and what we want to do. It takes determination to say no to things that get in the way of our self-care and yes to those that move us forward. That tension is part of our fabric. We will always confront peaks and valleys.

We learned a lot about the "wise mind" in chapter 3, "Therapy 101." Chip and Dan Heath, a dynamic duo of brothers,[64] have a great way of describing the wise mind, affirming many psychology research studies. They discuss how the rational side of our brains wants the beach body, while the emotional side wants the Oreo.[65] The constant battle between our rational and emotive minds makes it hard for us to budge. We want new results, but we're used to our usual routines and traditions. It takes time and effort to carve out new paths on which we can stay the course.

It's not uncommon for us to become discouraged when we have trouble sustaining our efforts. We all have off days, mental blocks, and times when it's difficult staying on top of our self-care. We compound

---

[64] Whatever their parents fed them for breakfast worked! Chip is blazing trails at Duke; Dan, at Stanford. Their *Switch: How to Change Things When Change is Hard* is a must-read.

[65] Did you hear the latest? Oreos are as addictive as cocaine! Hmm ... is this true whether you dunk, eat only the creamy middle, or eat only the top and bottom cookies?

the problem when we beat ourselves up and waste time chronicling all that we *haven't* done.

We stall out when we hyperfocus on weaknesses. Instead, it's important to focus on our strengths and on those areas for which we are equipped to make progress. As we discussed in chapter 3, building on our islands of competence improves our sense of self-efficacy—or belief in our own ability to complete tasks—and affirms our abilities. If we constantly focus on what's wrong or what we're failing to do, we lose precious time and energy.

An exception to this rule is for those of us who tend to be very laid back. In contrast to people who are obsessed with perfection, you may find yourself so lackadaisical that you make little to no progress. Your system may be understimulated, and you have trouble getting started. If this is the case, you need to crank up your expectations and develop a structure that leaves you little room to wriggle your way out. Very often, feedback from the people we care about, as hard as it can be to receive it, reveals where there is room to improve. Crafting a plan with building blocks will be necessary. Getting going can be very difficult; but without a reasonable plan, it becomes nearly impossible.

Looking for islands means scanning your resources for those that you can build upon. Remember the SWOT analyses you looked at earlier? Internal resources consist of such things as a sense of humor, self-awareness, and patience. External resources include family, colleagues, and community services. Internal resources, including your level of resilience, can be built upon. Hidden-gem external resources can be uncovered and developed once you start looking. When we look for what we need, we usually find it.

DISSECT AND REFLECT

- Do I believe change is possible?
- Am I hopeful and optimistic that I can improve my self-care?
- Have I faced a difficulty and implemented changes in certain areas of my life?
- If so, what was the catalyst?

- What types of things do I need to ask others to learn more about my strengths and most pronounced features?

> **BOTTOM LINE:** Change is difficult, but when we get stuck in the mire of believing it's not possible, we hinder our own growth. Look for possibilities, opportunities, and strengths and work to leverage them.

Measure it

While looking for islands, we can't ignore areas that need improvement. We all have weaknesses and challenges. We can either hide from them or get to the bottom of things.

It can be incredibly nerve wracking when we start taking inventory of our life conditions. We often live in denial, not wanting to absorb the truth of our circumstances. That's why we can hate looking at our bank account balances, stepping on the scale, or slowing down enough to think about what we're doing (or not doing). Sometimes we've tuned out for a long time, letting ourselves get to a pretty grim point. It's hard to acknowledge emotional strain, so we may run from it and pretend that we've got our acts together. This avoidance behavior can only hold up for so long.

When we're already stressed, the last thing we want is to feel that we are not doing a good job managing the pressure. But if we do not have a clear picture of where we are, we're in trouble. Knowing the truth may hurt at first but will be helpful in the long run.

There's something powerful about measurement. That premise is what makes Weight Watchers wildly successful, why companies invest a lot in pedometer programs for employees, and why apps that track our eating, sleep, and movement are increasingly used. More people than ever are seeking guidance from therapists, coaches, and mentors to give honest, pointed feedback that isn't sugarcoated. This phenomenon might have something to do with why Simon Cowell is so popular. Contestants on *American Idol* were able to make improvements based on his no-filter feedback. That kind of raw truth-telling may sting—but when we know where we stand, we can target our efforts more effectively.

Goals are developed according to baselines. Data is increasingly driving practices in education, medicine, social work, and the corporate world. We need a picture of what's happening now, in order to determine where we want to head. To enhance performance, we need to assess our current functioning and develop strategies tailored to us. This is true in our day-to-day lives, as well. In a moment, you'll have the chance to define your essential goals, but for now, you can start by reflecting on your baseline needs and priorities.

Without careful evaluation of what your total health looks like, it's impossible to develop a plan that will adequately address your needs. Implementing your RESET plan involves thoughtful assessment. Throughout this book, you've had the chance to dissect and reflect upon what you are already doing and to set goals for where you want to be. Even if you're not big on writing, documenting your goals in one way or another is an important start to reaching them.

Taking inventory will help you gauge where you need the most attention. As you'll see in phase 2 (below), when you define your essential goals, you will become more focused and strategic. This is a lot to accomplish, and self-measurements can often be skewed. This is where feedback comes in. By bringing help alongside, you can begin to develop a well-rounded picture of where you are.

Along those lines, one of the best gifts you can give to yourself is finding a therapist. Therapists are objective experts trained in self-care and stress. They are capable of evaluating needs and working to form constructive plans. The fact that therapeutic relationships are confidential is a huge help in reducing the inherent vulnerability in revealing ourselves and working toward change. Inviting loved ones into your process can also be beneficial, but sometimes there's nothing like having a neutral party to help with assessment and goal development.

> **Bottom Line:** While there are certain moments of truth we sometimes would rather not face, the answers provide us with valuable information needed to implement changes. The best place to start is by reviewing daily activities. Grab a notebook or your electronic device of choice and start taking note of where you are.

Dissect and Reflect

In order to evaluate your needs, start with doing a self-care check. Consider the five components of RESET:

Realize:

✓ Is this a particularly challenging time?

✓ What types of stressors am I facing?
  - Do my reactions seem proportional to the stressors I'm facing?
  - What will it take to develop resilience in light of the situations I am facing?

✓ What tends to trigger me?
  - Am I aware of those triggers during peak stress moments?

✓ When something goes wrong, do I allow enough time to regain perspective?

✓ Do I tend to make blanket judgments?

✓ Am I neglecting self-care?

✓ Am I paying attention to my context and factoring this into my perceptions of myself and others?
  - What are my work/home/school environments like, and what have they been like throughout my life?
  - What kind of resilience or difficulty runs in my family?

✓ Have I worked through similar moments before?

Energize:

- ✓ What's my health like?
- ✓ What is my body telling me?
- ✓ Am I getting enough movement?
- ✓ Are the foods and drinks I'm putting into my body helping me?
- ✓ Am I making time in my schedule to rest and relax?
- ✓ Do I get enough sleep?
- ✓ Is touch and affection part of my life?
- ✓ How often do I climax?
- ✓ What is my overall energy pulse?

Soothe:

- ✓ What are my favorite sensory experiences?
  - ○ What do I find soothing and stimulating?
  - ○ Is there anything I'm currently soothing myself with that is counterproductive to my RESET goals?
- ✓ Are there any sensory triggers I need to account for?
- ✓ How can I make my environment more appealing?
  - ○ Is there anyone who can help me with this?
- ✓ Am I paying enough attention to the way I am breathing and holding my body?
- ✓ What changes do I need to institute?

End unproductive thinking

- ✓ Am I paying attention to my appraisal process?
- ✓ What percentage of time am I engrossed in productive versus unproductive thinking?
- ✓ Are there opportunities to learn that I can start participating in?
- ✓ What is my mantra?
- ✓ What else can I add in my self-talk repertoire to help me stay positive and productive?

Talk it out:

- ✓ Who are my supports?

   ○ What are my current relationships like?
   ○ Do I need to ask others for more or less of what they are doing?
  ✓ Do I have a therapist or coach to help me?
  ✓ Is there anyone in my reach who would make a great mentor?
  ✓ What activities will help me build additional connections?

BOTTOM LINE: A launch point is needed to improve well-being. Assessing various dimensions of our health can help with pinpointing areas that need the most attention. Having a baseline is a *critical* step in any change effort.

Phase 1 in a Nutshell

Evaluate:
What's Working Well, and What's Not?

1. **You *can* teach an old dog new tricks**
    *   Change, while not a linear process, is possible.
    *   We can evolve and progress over time.

2. **Look for islands**
    *   Our rational and emotive minds are often in conflict.
    *   Pushing ourselves to change is delicate—we don't want to be either too intense or too laid back while we implement our RESET plan.
    *   Uncovering hidden-gem resources within and outside of ourselves is key.
    *   When we look for resources, we usually find them.

3. **Measure it!**
    *   We have to acknowledge our shortcomings, health status, and other life variables in order to develop an effective plan.
    *   Taking inventory helps us construct a sustainable plan.

PHASE 2

PRIORITIZE: SET TARGET GOALS

> Action is the antidote to despair.
> —Joan Baez

ESSENTIAL QUESTION: Are there pressing areas in my life in which I am experiencing burnout, and what structure can help me take immediate action?

Define the essentials

Self-care strategies are endless. There are so many variations that it can be overwhelming to know where to begin. If we try to tackle too much all at once, we might stall out. If we aren't ambitious enough, what we do won't have enough effect on our stress bottom line.

Sometimes we get stuck over the very notion of self-care because we think it won't help or that we are being selfish even to consider taking care of ourselves. Many of us, in a noble attempt to help others, end up neglecting ourselves and then find ourselves overwhelmed and burned out. Burnout isn't a joke. If we're in a professional or personal role where we are responsible for others, this cranks up the burnout risk substantially. Parents, teachers, doctors, managers, nurses, social workers, psychologists, clergy, and any type of caregiver—among many other professions and roles—need to take self-care very seriously. Basically, if you have anyone who relies on you in some capacity, it makes your own self-care all the more important. Many of us have *multiple* roles that involve supporting others, so self-care becomes even more essential. Burnout can lead to many negative consequences for not only ourselves, but those we care for.

Term	Definition	CONSIDER THIS
Burnout	Syndrome of emotional exhaustion, depersonalization, and reduced accomplishment; burnout leads to becoming withdrawn and worn out, which affects our relationships and performance.	When we are working with others in any capacity, we run the risk of getting depleted from the stress this can bring. Self-care helps reduce the chances of getting too frazzled.

Ironically, when burnout occurs, we lose our ability to be responsive to those around us and fulfill our roles. At work and school, our performance suffers when we don't make time to regroup and recalibrate.

When we set boundaries and make time for self-care, we're doing a service for more than just ourselves. When we're well rested, nurtured, and energetic, this translates into our being happier, more positive, more receptive and capable, and more fun to be around.

Everyone deserves to have a self-care regimen. Even if you find it difficult to define a few essential areas for your own self-care, I hope you will give yourself permission to try.

> **Bottom Line:** When we devote our time and attention to everyone and everything but ourselves, we're heading down a slippery slope. It's not selfish to invest in self-care but rather a way to ensure that we stay well enough to fulfill our roles, which is more possible when we're at our best.

In the next section, you'll develop goals that are based on your own needs. For now, it's important to stop and reflect on the most pressing issues you are facing and to develop some priorities.

You've already started to evaluate what's working well and what needs some attention. Based on your assessment, consider what you have uncovered that is/are vital to your health and happiness. Are there any glaring aspects that stand out and that you simply can no longer choose to overlook? If so, it will be important to develop goals with very specific steps to help you progress.

Here are some signs that stress may be wreaking havoc in your life:

- You're not smiling and laughing much (and are possibly crying more).
- Your work or academic performance is shaky, disrupted, and/ or you find your concentration and focus aren't as sharp as usual.
- You have high reliance on prescription or illicit drugs, need for more caffeine, alcohol, or other measures to keep your energy levels up and/or stress levels manageable.
- Relationships are tumultuous or difficult to maintain; people seem concerned about, frustrated with, or disappointed in you.
- You are experiencing feelings of fatigue/exhaustion, trouble getting going, low energy, achiness, and/or difficulty following through with usual routines.
- You have appetite/weight increases or decreases; your body frame is too thin, too heavy, or your system is thrown off-kilter.
- You have decreased interest in things you once enjoyed or found interesting; you are experiencing withdrawal, less passion, isolation, and even cynicism.

- You are experiencing irritability or moodiness and have a short fuse; you are snappy with yourself or others and have low tolerance levels.
- You are revved up, anxious, filled with adrenaline, high strung, and in constant overdrive.
- You have panic attacks, a racing heart, shortness of breath, heightened fears, and/or sensory overload.
- You have trouble seeing future as optimistic, lack of hopefulness, lack of planning or goal setting
- You exhibit physical signs like hair loss, low immune system (always getting sick), acne/breakouts, dark circles under eyes, and lackluster skin.

This is quite a list to consider and will help you to narrow down your essential priorities. If you find yourself identifying with several of these stress signs, hopefully you'll feel compelled to take immediate action. Consider what is taking the greatest toll on you and what it would mean for you if it were improved. Talk to trusted family and friends to see if they have any concerns. Try to listen without overreacting, and gather as much information as possible. Think of yourself as your own health detective, on a quest to find out what you need most. This takes a certain measure of strength, but being defensive will only get in the way of your self-care planning.

As you begin to define your priorities, you will notice that it will require time and effort to begin changing your existing routines. It will become apparent that you need to manage your time well. Structuring time—whether you are wildly busy or have only a few responsibilities—will be a critical element for success.

Next, see if you can make a connection with what you're experiencing and the context in which you're operating. Some major sources of stress typically include the following:

- work or academic performance
- health
- finances

- relationships
- loss
- trauma/abuse

Using this chart as a guide, see if you can pick a few key areas to start brainstorming about. Here are some examples to get you thinking:

What I know about myself (insights)	What I need to do (system)?	Things that get in the way (roadblocks)	Things that help me (facilitators)
Example 1 My grandmother's death has been hard on me. I'm not myself, and I haven't been socializing much lately.	I'm not comfortable being around a lot of people, but I'm going to pick a friend to walk with on Mondays, Wednesdays, and Fridays.	My work schedule, weather, and lack of motivation and energy.	Asking my friend to be firm in holding me to the commitment, remembering how important this is to my self-care routine, giving myself time during the week to grieve and regroup.
Example 2 My work schedule is so busy that I am eating way too much junk food.	I have to plan ahead and make sure I buy bagged salads and healthy soups. On the weekends, I can cook extra and take leftovers with me.	Getting distracted, lots of fast-food places are on my route to work, carb cravings are hard to resist, forgetfulness.	Using grocery delivery service or having a set day to pick up food when there's more time to prepare it and pack it up, finding healthy to-go snacks and meals online, hanging out with friends who are on a similar quest.

Example 3			
Whenever something goes wrong, I blame myself and get very discouraged. I get to the point where I feel I hate myself and even those around me.	This pattern started early on for me. I have to avoid spending too much time thinking and dissecting myself. When I stay busy and engaged in positive projects and with people, I feel better.	My habits have existed for years. If I hang around with certain people, it just reinforces my self-sabotage tendencies. When I spend too much time alone, especially during the winter months, I get depressed.	I plan to join a gym during the winter and volunteer at the food pantry. Giving to others helps them and also helps me. My new mantra is "I'm doing my best." I will remind myself of this every time the negative thoughts creep in.

Don't delay. It seems to be human nature to procrastinate. But when we let ourselves get saturated with stress, this should be taken seriously. Maintaining emotional health has a profoundly positive effect on our physical health and total well-being. When we really think about it, we wouldn't dream of putting off things that are far less important. If we wait to begin our self-care efforts, we not only waste valuable time in improving our lives but also risk allowing our situations to deteriorate. We should avoid delay at all costs.

And the wonderful fact is that, with self-care, once small changes are instituted, we feel an almost immediate, positive impact.

Now that you've started to consider your essential areas to target, it's time to carve out a concrete plan of action.

Map it out

The advent of the GPS, Google Maps, and scouting applications have been a true godsend, especially if you're directionally challenged, as I am. Without a map, we stumble and lose our way.

This is no different in the self-care realm. We need a map to guide us, particularly in following through on matters that impact our emotional and physical well-being.

All too often, once we evaluate what we are doing (or not doing), we set up elaborate goals that don't really fit us, or we set vague and open-ended goals that we soon put on the back burner. Soon after, we're kicking ourselves for not following through—even though the design, by its nature, was a setup for failure.

Designing the right goals helps us develop a road map for well-being. The concept of SMART goals has been widely discussed in project management, corporate functioning, and personal development. Since the time it was originally proposed, *ER* has been added to allow for revision and to help promote lasting impact. The first step in establishing SMARTER goals is to nail down your change effort.

Start by asking yourself the five **W**'s:

- **What:** What exactly do I need to accomplish?
- **Why:** Why is this important to my well-being?
- **Who:** Who do I need to help me carry this forth?
- **Where:** Where will I accomplish this?
- **Which:** Which type of requirements and constraints do I face?

Your answers will help you home in on what is most essential in your self-care plan. When developing your RESET goals, this is an excellent framework to help get you started:

Term	Definition	CONSIDER THIS
S—Specific	Helps us answer the "5 W's" and narrow our focus in a clear, compelling manner.	Drilling down and getting to a high level of specificity helps us develop a concrete plan.
M—Measurable	Gives us traction as we monitor goal-attainment progress in number terms, such as "How many/much?"	It's hard to know if we're making progress without measurement. It helps us stay focused and on task and is motivating when we see proof that we've reached our goals.
A—Attainable	Ensures that a goal is balanced, will be meaningful enough to have impact, and won't overwhelm us. Focuses on the question of "How?"	When we develop attainable goals, it helps promote focus and follow-through. They help us picture success and create a path toward it.
R—Relevant	Helps provide assurance that what we're doing matters to our self-care progress. Helps us answer "Is it the time for this?" and "Does this fit with my needs?"	The more relevant, the better. Obscure goals that we don't connect with are hard to follow.

T—Time-bound	Pinpoints a target date of completion to prevent goals from being put on the back burner. Helps distinguish pressing needs and answers the question "When?"	Deadlines have a way of kicking us into gear. Having a sense of urgency keeps motivation and focus in the forefront.
E—Evaluate	Gives us the opportunity to go back to the drawing board and determine if our design needs tweaking. Evaluating our efforts helps answer "Is what I'm doing working?"	Assessment informs growth and helps us tailor our approaches. When we reflect upon what we're doing, we are more likely to continue to develop goals that will have maximum impact.
R—Revise	Establishes new strategies to boost effectiveness. Helps us craft new plans based on what we have learned thus far. Answers the questions "What else is possible" and "What will work even better?"	There's no shame in having to make adjustments to original plans. This is, in fact, an excellent way to nail down a plan that leads to maximum impact.

Here is an example of a goal targeted at getting more sleep. Using this as a guide, you'll have a chance to construct a similar chart for three of your own goals.

Component:	Pinpoint and describe:
What	My goal is to increase my sleep by one hour, for a total of eight per night.
Why	Sleep is essential for brain and body recovery, and I notice I've been dragging at work.
Who	I am responsible for carrying this forth. I can delegate some of my responsibilities to other family members and ask that the house quiets down by a certain time.
Where	At home.
Which	I will need to manage my time better and modify my existing routines. With a busy schedule, I will have to practice stopping work by 9:00 p.m. in order to start transitioning to my bedtime routine.

I recommend using this framework as a way to start constructing goals. Start by thinking about *maximum impact*. What areas of your well-being have you noticed affect you the most? To start, look at the biggies like sleep, diet, and exercise.

This doesn't need to be overly sophisticated or elaborate. If scratching your plan on a sticky note or a napkin is your preferred method, then start there. The key is *starting*, based on what you really need, now, to begin making changes and improvements.

> **BOTTOM LINE:** The SMARTER goals framework is practical and provides an excellent structure for your RESET plan. Start with one or two areas, and break them out into constructive, concrete, manageable parts.

Enlist support

Once you've got your priorities and goals established, it is important to connect with others who will work with you and hold you accountable. That's why people work out together, study in groups, and form project teams. When we know people are counting on us, we're more likely to follow through. We need community to propel us forward.

Knowing that we're in the same boat with others is also a tremendous help. I can tell you that any struggle you may be having—whether of a motivational nature or something else—is not unique to you. We sometimes get tricked into thinking that we're the *only* ones who have trouble with certain things; but in fact, our responses and feelings are more similar to other people's than we may realize.

Enlisting support can mean that you invite people to participate in specific self-care activities to keep you company or to help keep you on track with your goals. You can join me on my website, RESET24-7. com to join the conversation with others who are also striving towards well-being. There is power in knowing we're in this together.

Another form of support comes when you delegate some of your responsibilities to make time for your self-care. If you're like me, you have a little martyr in you, and you try to do it all without asking for help. If we're to stay healthy and invested in self-care, we may need to rethink our overly individualistic, by-our-bootstraps mind-sets. Part of a thoughtful self-care plan involves defining the essential things we must handle and what can be delegated. This is true both in teamwork and in relationships. There are some things we're better at and can take the lead on. In other situations, our friends, families, and partners are better equipped to take the lead. Setting up a support system can lead to higher efficiency and happiness.

> **Bottom Line:** If there are things you are not good at or simply do not have time to accomplish, don't be afraid to enlist the support of someone who has the resources to help you along. Stay in your own lane, and avoid swerving all over the place trying to please everyone and be good at everything. We end up losing valuable time and energy otherwise.

Dissect and Reflect

- What types of tasks can I delegate to reduce my load and allow more time for self-care?
- Who is part of my current support system?
- Is there someone I can enlist, professionally or personally, to come alongside me for added support?
- Using the chart below, pick a goal to start working on immediately:

Component:	Pinpoint and describe:
What	
Why	
Who	
Where	
Which	

- Who will I enlist to help me with this goal?
- What conversations on RESET24-7.com are most pertinent to me? How will I take this and move forward in my goals?

> **Bottom Line:** Self-care is not an individual endeavor. You can't do this alone. Don't even try!

Phase 2 in a Nutshell

Prioritize:
Set Target Goals

1. **Define the essentials**
   - Self-care strategies are endless; examining our most pressing health issues is vital.
   - Self-care is not a selfish endeavor.
   - Burnout is no joke. People who are in the role of caring for others—whether professionally or personally—are at a high risk from burnout, and they would benefit from the anchor of a well-constructed self-care plan.
   - Our bodies' signs and symptoms are worth listening to.
   - Identifying insights, systems, roadblocks, and facilitators helps us pinpoint priorities.
   - When something is counterproductive to your RESET plan, work to reduce or eliminate it.

2. **Map it out**
   - The SMARTER goals framework helps us to develop a concrete plan of action.
   - Pick your essential needs, and start mapping out a plan that best suits you.

3. **Enlist support**
   - Engaging in self-care with others helps hold us accountable and promotes follow-through. RESET24-7. com offers supportive conversation with others striving towards well-being.
   - Delegating responsibilities helps us clear the way for more self-care.

PHASE 3

IMPLEMENT: BRING YOUR RESET PLAN TO LIFE

Motivation is what gets you started.
Habit is what keeps you going.
—Jim Rohn

ESSENTIAL QUESTION: What daily practices will help me maintain momentum and follow-through?

Get bang for your buck

When we're already up and running, swirling from one activity to the next, it's worth seeing where we can piggyback our efforts. Instead of making a long list of Hail-Mary goals, start by paying attention to what can naturally or easily be slipped in. Often, things can be added to our self-care regimens that fit in nicely with what we're already doing. These can be simple: adding one more workout to our week, adjusting how far away we park at our destination, plugging in an audiobook during a long commute, tossing in a handful of spinach to the fruit smoothie we're already making. When we are constantly looking for *maximum* impact within out daily routines, we often find bring lots of opportunities for momentum building.

Now that you've learned the RESET principles, see if you can nail down activities that hit on multiple aspects. For example, get in the habit of meeting with people over a walk instead of over food. These "walk/talks" can be enjoyable and kill two birds with one stone, addressing the Energize and Talk It Out components simultaneously. When you craft your RESET plan, consider what types of activities reach into more than one area. Here are some of my favorites:

- **Reading on the treadmill** (Energize, End Unproductive Thinking)
- **Swimming at the beach** (Energize, Soothe)
- **Watching documentaries** (Energize, End Unproductive Thinking)
- **Exploring natures trails with loved ones** (Energize, Soothe, Talk It Out)
- **Prayer and solitude** (Realize, Energize, Soothe, End Unproductive Thinking)

As you can see, this is just the beginning of virtually endless possibilities. It's wise to consider maximum impact as you develop your activities. Sometimes it's just too difficult to start from scratch or try to do lofty things that bring us far out of our way or put too many additional demands on us. Small things can make a big difference. Keep exploring what makes sense given your comings and goings, and sneak in self-care every chance you get! Maybe you can pray while driving, sing in the shower, or chat with a friend over a steaming mug of tea. The key is being deliberate about your efforts before, during, and after. It's important to reinforce this message continually: *all* forms of self-care help make the most of your stress—and enable you to anchor down the benefits of what you're doing.

Watch out for double whammies

Just as it's worth looking for positive activities that address multiple levels of our self-care regimen, we have to watch out for ones that pack a punch in unfavorable ways. Instead of anchoring ourselves down emotionally, we may end up engaging in activities that are counterproductive to our self-care and health. Just as it's important to think about getting bang for our buck when it comes to positive activities, we have to consider the impact on the converse side of things. Hangouts consisting of excess alcohol, greasy food, and co-rumination with friends who drag us down can seriously get in the way of our self-care. We have to be careful that we're not only engaging in adaptive measures but also avoiding maladaptive, toxic activities, relationships, and patterns.

> **Bottom Line:** Our well-being is complex. The various factors that influence it are often intertwined. Sometimes when we address one issue, it gives us better stamina, allowing us to make changes in more than one area. If you already are doing X, then why not add Y? Similarly, watch out for areas that may be causing a double-negative impact.

Dissect and Reflect

- What types of activities lend themselves to adding on other means of self-care?
- What types of double dips and piggybacking can I engage in for maximum self-care impact?
- What might I need to cut out and avoid to minimize disruption to my positive efforts?

Be flexible

Even with careful planning and the best of intentions, sometimes things just don't work out as well as we'd hoped. It may take more than a few tries to get into the right rhythm. There are a host of reasons for this. Sometimes we get discouraged and develop an all-or-nothing mind-set. We may start out full tilt with our RESET goals and then end up with them on the back burner. This is human. Sometimes we're plain bored. Adding novelty may help refocus us. Other times, things are too complex, and life just takes over. Injuries, loss, and the unexpected happen, seriously getting in the way of what we've set out to do. The fear of fizzling out is actually a good thing. It keeps us motivated to work on our discipline to keep from stalling out.

Creating a self-care plan is a fluid process. Our plans will evolve and change over time. When barriers get in the way of our efforts, we need to create new paths. Rather than giving up, we've got to press forward, avoiding the tendency to get frustrated to the point of quitting. It's important to realize that this is not about instant gratification but about sculpting a long-term plan that can enable us to change some of our basic thought and behavior patterns. We may have to go back to the drawing board more than once to get it right.

> **Bottom Line:** Flexibility is key when implementing your RESET plan. Self-care is complex, since our needs and resources are constantly in flux. Because change is the only constant in life, we need to stay nimble and optimistic even when things don't go according to plan. Over time, and with practice, we develop resilience and grit to help us stay consistent and focused.

Dissect and Reflect:

- Are my expectations realistic?
- Have I crafted SMARTER goals that fit well with my essential needs?

- Who or what will help me remember to stay flexible if things don't go as planned?

24-7 self-care

Our humanness comprises many wonders and complexities. As strong as we are, we require maintenance to endure the trials of life. Just as our cars run of gas and our bodies need continual food and water, our emotional tanks are also in constant need of refueling. We wouldn't dream of trying to go across country on empty or of going days without eating or drinking—yet lots of times we push ourselves to the emotional limits, forgetting to fuel up and regroup.

I recently came across this quote that illustrates the nature of life and importance of self-care as a tool for constant recalibration and perspective taking:

> A lot of things are inherent in life—change, birth, death, aging, illness, accidents, calamities, and losses of all kinds— but these events don't have to be the cause of ongoing suffering. Yes, these events cause grief and sadness, but grief and sadness pass, like everything else, and are replaced with other experiences. The ego, however, clings to negative thoughts and feelings and, as a result, magnifies, intensifies, and sustains those emotions while the ego overlooks the subtle feelings of joy, gratitude, excitement, adventure, love, and peace that come from Essence. If we dwelt on these positive states as much as we generally dwell on our negative thoughts and painful emotions, our lives would be transformed.[66]

Because life is so complex, with uncertainties looming, we have to be steadfast in keeping our emotions in check and working continually on self-care. It's hard work, and as we've learned, it's not

---

[66] Lake, Gina. *What about Now?: Reminders for Being in the Moment*. Sedona: Dreamstime, 2009.

just reserved for crises. The RESET principles, in fact, work best when we're constantly using them.

In order to make the most of our stress, we need to take deliberate action. Burnout is no joke. If we're only investing meager amounts of time and energy into our well-being, we'll fade much more quickly than we'd like. When we completely ignore warning signs that we are losing traction, the results can prove disastrous. Physical, emotional, and mental resilience hinge on our attention to these signs. While no specific formula can give us this resilience, conscientiously using a program such as RESET helps to build this resilience in a variety of ways.

Stress is a constant. We all have some version we are dealing with and in varying intensities throughout the seasons of our lives. Recalibration is something that we will always require, particularly if we want to be able to harness our strengths along with the aspects of stress that give us momentum.

It's hard to remember all this when we're in the throes of distress. For years, information about our emotional health and mental functioning has been convoluted and laden with a blaming tone. We haven't been conditioned to be proactive in looking for our strengths and resources. Many of us are hard on ourselves and constantly seek more success, recognition, and golden tickets in one form or another. We end up paying a high price when we forget to make the time to reframe and regroup.

Since we only have one live to life, it's worth making sure that we're investing in our body, mind, and spirit. Self-care needs to be a priority. Nothing is worth the trade-off of our mental well-being. While we possess the capacity for amazing levels of resilience, we can't take it for granted that we'll bounce back if we've done nothing to contribute to that resilience. When we tend to ourselves, we are more likely to enjoy our lives, remain resilient, and contribute positively to others. Doing so is well worth the investment!

> **BOTTOM LINE:** Stress is a constant and demands our attention. Our 24-7 self-care helps us remain resilient through the inevitable twists and turns that we face during various seasons of life. The RESET principles are a guide to help you stay calibrated and in tune as you work toward your goals for total well-being.

Celebrating the many changes made along the trails, here are some simple yet inspirational examples of RESET experienced by people I know.

Brie's story

Brie noticed that her commute was really eating at her and took too much time away from her already-marginless schedule. Her thought process was far from productive while she sat in traffic, and she often felt her entire body tensing from head to toe. With no end in sight, she decided to start listening to positive books while driving. This proved to be extremely helpful, and she built quite a repertoire of tapes of coping strategies and inspiration to use in the car and beyond.

Benny's story

Mornings were just rough for Benny. He hit snooze until the last minute and frantically ran around to get himself out of the house on time. This usually meant no breakfast and a flared temper, and it set a negative tone for his busy workday. Benny was a night owl and had trouble getting to sleep at night. He decided that his morning madness was growing old and thought about what would make a difference. He resolved to revise his night routines to take his dog for a walk earlier and to prepare his lunch and iron his clothes ahead of time for the next day. This reorganization made a difference. Mornings weren't perfect, but they got a lot better. Benny's small changes led to more organization at home, and he noticed over time that this made him more relaxed and at ease.

Jorge's story

Jorge's ruminations were epic and pervasive. He could barely shut his mind off, and at the urging of his therapist, he wore a small red rubber band on his wrist. He gently snapped it each time an intrusive thought came to the surface. He then tallied it in his phone. Over the course of a week, Jorge had logged over 233 negative thoughts! By measuring it, he realized that he would need to engage in various forms of RESET to help him overcome this strong tide within him. Jorge enrolled in a yoga class and sought the help of an acupuncturist. Almost immediately, he felt able to engage in more productive, positive thinking.

What will your change(s) be?

Join the conversation at http://www.RESET24-7.com

Phase 3 in a Nutshell

Implement:
Bring Your RESET Plan to Life

1. **Get bang for your buck**
   - Instead of making Hail Mary–pass goals, examine what you're already doing and what can be piggybacked on.
   - Work to hit more than one RESET principle in your activities.

2. **Be flexible**
   - Self-care is a dynamic, fluid process that changes with our needs.
   - Starting and stalling is human. Keep enough fear to stay motivated, but be patient with yourself.
   - Head back to the drawing board when necessary.

3. **24-7 self-care**
   - There are complexities and wonders in being human.
   - We need constant refueling and recalibration.
   - Our activities either fit in with our self-care plan, or they do not.
   - Self-care is a continual, 24-7, lifelong process worth investing in.

APPENDIX A

RESET in Review

Realize:

Identify magnifiers and triggers and realize that "peak stress moments" are simply not the time to make blanket judgments. Remember that your "first take" or primary appraisal usually needs revision. Give yourself time, and go back to the drawing board. The "second take" allows you to reframe and gain traction.

Energize:

Pick at least two or three new activities or habits to add to your repertoire. Consider reducing two or three aspects of your life that drag you down and work to change them. Fuel up, regroup, connect, and keep moving!

Soothe:

Change something in your environment or routine. Deliberately absorb this using your senses. Take time to delight in sensory experiences, and comfort your mind, body, and spirit when you are oversaturated. Work at adaptive soothing as much as possible to help prevent tendencies toward maladaptive measures. Listen to your body!

End unproductive thinking:
Pay attention to the way you are appraising situations, and engage your mind in productive thinking and endeavors. Seek learning opportunities, and engage with activities that are positive and constructive. Draw upon a personal mantra as you coach yourself through challenging moments.

Talk it out:
Evaluate your relationships, and make sure that you are connected. Seek therapeutic people, including others who have similar and different vantage points. Be sure that you are debriefing your stress and not bottling it up. Avoid isolation. We can't do this alone.

Recommendations for Further Growth

Acupuncture

Dubbed "the fastest growing health care treatment" in the United States, acupuncture is here to stay. We are finally catching up with what Eastern cultures have practiced for centuries. Acupuncture can provide a wonderful RESET by helping to increase the flow of *qi*, or energy, in our bodies. Some insurance plans cover treatments, and many community acupuncture centers offer reduced-cost sessions based on ability to pay.

Art

Engaging in artistic activity, either as an artist or appreciator, can be highly beneficial. Art taps into our creative side, allowing us to express ourselves beyond words and gestures. Art therapy is a modality known to be highly therapeutic. Check to see what types of classes, crafting, galleries, and shows are offered in your community. Libraries often have free passes to museums and related events.

Coaching

The use of life coaches has grown exponentially over the past decade for good reason. Coaching intends to motivate and keep us accountable with follow-through. Coaches help with outside-the-box thinking and remind us when we're taking too many detours away from our goals.

Coaches focus on life and professional strategies and also assist in a wide range of areas that involve maximizing our potential.

Chiropractic care
A chiropractor can help reset your spine and body systems, which can do a world of good. Ask your primary care provider or health insurance company, or do some local research to find someone with a solid reputation.

Community resources and services
Oftentimes, our communities are rich with resources that we may not know exist. It's worth keeping your eyes peeled for a range of support groups that can remind us that we're not alone and give us hope in regard to all sorts of issues. A great way to track them down is by using the United Way's 2-1-1 information line, which is devoted to providing free and confidential referrals specifically around food, housing, employment, health care, counseling, and more: http://www.211.org/

Craniosacral therapy
Performed often by chiropractors, this modality is nothing short of extraordinary. This gentle treatment method targets the central nervous system and helps release tensions deep within the body.

Community and social connections
Would you like to add some more friends to your social circle? Pay attention to what's happening at your local churches and community centers, and seek out opportunities for events or activities that are appealing to you. Many clubs are out there to be joined: board game, book, walking, pet lovers, and many more. A great website that helps you track them down is http://www.meetup.com/.

Personal insight and self-awareness tools
SWOT analyses, 360-degree feedback, personality tests, and the like help us learn more about how others perceive us. We can ask questions of ourselves, therapists, coaches, friends, family, and colleagues to bolster our emotional intelligence and ensure that we are behaving

according to our values and that others can see evidence of this. There's a wealth of information in this vein online.

Massage

Once thought of as an indulgence, massage is now being seen as a powerful force in health maintenance. As *Oprah* magazine once noted, "Massage isn't just for blissing out." Besides being thoroughly relaxing, massage stimulates our oxytocin levels, promoting bonding, empathy, and other spectacular warm fuzzies (or something like that). Massage is recognized in helping stave off inflammation, high blood pressure, and autoimmune conditions. There are various types, so be sure to find one based on your own preference and needs. Shiatsu massage in particular is known to trigger serotonin levels and to invoke pure elation. Massage schools offer discounted fees, and some places have sliding-scale fees. Online coupons or package deals are also ways to keep the costs in check.

Music

Music invokes powerful emotions and is often the backdrop of our lives. Careful selection can make a world of difference in the realm of self-care. Whether you are an avid listener or a musician, you know how beneficial music is to our emotional and physical health. Singing (or even humming) can be a great mood booster. Check your community for local concerts, coffee houses, performances, and the like.

Neurofeedback

This technique is gaining a lot of attention and becoming recognized as an excellent mode of treatment targeted at recalibrating brain and body responses. Neurofeedback practitioners have long known the benefit of helping the brain function at its best, particularly if someone is struggling with disruptions associated with anxiety, depression spectrum, ADD/ADHD, and more. EEG Education and Research, Inc. is a great place to learn more: http://www.eegspectrum. com/intro-to-neurofeedback/

Psychotherapy

Gone are the days of Freud and couches. Today's therapy is solution focused and goal driven. Therapy can benefit any of us—whether we're working to adjust to a life change or completely saturated in stress. Having an objective, confidential person in your life that is cheering you on and wanting the best for you can mean everything. It's important to find someone you click with.

Make sure that your therapist is licensed and experienced, particularly in the areas you are looking to focus upon. Besides asking someone who seems really happy, it's a good idea to check with such professional associations as the National Association of Social Workers http://www.nasw.org/ or the American Psychological Association www.apa.org for top-notch recommendations.

You can also ask your primary care physician or health insurance company to help you find someone who suits your needs. It's worth taking the time to research someone who is recommended, and if you're uneasy after the first visit, keep looking. Finding a good fit is very important. While clinical social workers, psychologists, and mental health clinicians are able to assess medication needs, further assessment by a psychiatrist may be needed. Only MDs and CNPs (certified nurse practitioners) can prescribe medication.

NOTE: If you are in a crisis or emergency emotional state, it is best to go to your local crisis center for evaluation and recommendations based on your unique care needs.

Support groups and twelve-step programs

There are a wealth of anonymous twelve-step programs and support groups for virtually any issue and cause imaginable. From gambling to overeating to sexual addictions and more, support exists. You can easily find these online; additionally, primary care physicians and wellness practitioners are often up on what's available in your area. If you have an individual therapist, she or he can help you find something suitable near you. NAMI, http://nami.org, and CHADD, http://www.chadd.org/, are just two of many options. You can also Google twelve-step programs to find more.

Volunteer

Giving of your time to help others is a wonderful way to contribute to our world. In addition to helping those around us, it helps us keeps perspective and remain engaged and upbeat. When we lend a hand, it makes a difference. You can find volunteer opportunities by paying attention to needs around you and by visiting: http://www. volunteermatch.org/.

Writing

Writing is a powerful tool to help us with processing, goal setting, and communicating. Writing can activate our creative juices and be an energizing, transformative process. There are often community classes and groups to sign up for, and many therapists use their clients' writing as a tool to bolster treatment progress.

Spiritual development

A universal truth across various faiths is "Love your neighbor"—not a bad place to start. For many of us, this is in alignment with our moral code, and now research is affirming that one gains a real health benefit in serving others. When we focus less on ourselves and forge connections that lift the human spirit, it's highly beneficial to everyone. Finding our purpose and connection to something greater than ourselves can be enlightening. Prayer, reading scripture, reflecting, and meditation are all spiritual practices that can help us develop and devote ourselves to a higher calling and purpose. Spiritual people have known this for ages, and now research is catching up and affirming it, with evidence that people who pray and attend church have lower stress levels and higher life satisfaction.

Exercise/athletic endeavors

There are many free and low-cost options right at your back door. From joining your local YMCA to walking with a neighbor to joining a walking club to swimming in your local public pool, you can find tons of options. Scan your environment to see what piques your interest and go for it! Try spinning, tai chi, aerobics, or cardio-lifting, and see what you enjoy.

Personal organizers

One of my favorite book titles of all time is *A Housekeeper is Cheaper Than a Divorce*. Not everyone has a knack for cleaning. Some of us weren't born with a bottle of Windex in hand, and we need to enlist the help of someone who has the touch. Clutter and unclean living environments can be a sign of emotional unrest, and they become draining and overwhelming for those living with lots of messes. If this is true for you, it's not a moral failing on your part—you just need some help. A sign that you're not alone is the rising number of online resources, cleaning/organizing services, and maybe even the hoarding reality shows.

Learning, intellectual, and professional development

We covered this in greater detail in the "Learn, Baby, Learn" section of chapter 11: "End Unproductive Thinking," but it's worth repeating these excellent resources to keep your growth and inspiration active:

- **EdX:** https://www.edx.org/
- **Ted Talks:** http://www.ted.com/
- **Toastmasters International:** http://www.toastmasters.org/
- **Professional organizations:** Type your profession into Google for ideas.
- **Your local library:** Between the books, DVDs, and events, you'll benefit greatly from your library's offerings. Take advantage of interlibrary loaning, a wonderful system that delivers your order to your nearest library for easy pickup.

Performing arts

There's nothing like a live dance, theatrical, or musical performance to stimulate our senses and tap into our creative sides. Ben Cameron's TED Talk that shares his passion for performing arts is persuasive and powerful. Getting out and immersing yourself in different artistic media can be truly wonderful. Check out local performances. Ask about student, senior, military, and matinee discounts.

Entertainment

Whether it's a sitcom or movie of today or a classic from the past, we all have our favorites that make us roar and evoke sheer joy. Sitting back and enjoying something entertaining gives our minds a diversion from the grind of our day-to-day responsibilities. Sometimes we just need to zone out or engross ourselves in something riveting or just plain funny.

Recommended Reading

While writing RESET, I read just about every self-help and personal development book I could get my hands on (both popular and clinical). In fact, I'm convinced that my librarians are officially concerned. Here's a sample of my enduring favorites. If you like *RESET*, you'll love the following:

✓ ***Daring Greatly: How the Courage to Be Vulnerable Transforms the Way We Live, Love, Parent, and Lead*** by Brené Brown
Dr. Brown brings together years of research and practice to present a compelling case toward working through uncertainty, risk, and emotional exposure in order to live more freely and authentically. *Daring Greatly* reminds us of the importance of curbing the tendency to want to mask our vulnerabilities and instead step into "the arena" with great courage and conviction.

✓ ***Crazy Busy: Overstretched, Overbooked, and About to Snap! Strategies for Handling Your Fast-Paced Life*** by Edward Hallowell
Dr. Hallowell captures the essence of modern-day scurry in a way that makes you think he is a fly on the wall in your own crazy, busy life. He shows us how the world is ADD/ADHD and helps us make deliberate choices about how to respond to the nonstop demands tossed at us: http://www.drhallowell.com/crazy-busy/

✓ *David and Goliath: Underdogs, Misfits, and the Art of Battling Giants* by Malcolm Gladwell
In true form, Gladwell gives us another delightful read as he demonstrates how underdogs can win and why setbacks and obstacles aren't necessarily as harmful as we often make them out to be. Visit http://gladwell.com/ for this and his other extraordinary offerings.

✓ *Focus: The Hidden Driver of Excellence* by Daniel Goleman
Dr. Goleman offers inspiration on sustaining our attention in our ultradistracted world. He encourages readers to rely on specific practices to excel in all areas of performance; see http://www.danielgoleman.info/ to learn more.

✓ *Mindset: The New Psychology of Success* by Carol Dweck
Like fine wine and cheese, Dr. Dweck's work keeps getting better over time. Devoting her life to research and practice, her framing of "growth mindsets" is inspirational and helpful as we work to build on our abilities throughout our lives: http://mind-setonline.com/.

✓ *The Dance of Connection: How to Talk to Someone When You're Mad, Hurt, Scared, Frustrated, Insulted, Betrayed, or Desperate* by Harriet Lerner
An oldie but goodie, this classic book, among Dr. Lerner's many others with similar titles, helps highlight communication practices that lead to more authentic and meaningful relationships. Her take on "overfunctioners" is especially helpful if you tend to take on too much. You can find more about her work at http://www.harrietlerner.com/.

✓ *The Happiness Project: Or, Why I Spent a Year Trying to Sing in the Morning, Clean My Closets, Fight Right, Read Aristotle, and Generally Have More Fun* by Gretchin Rubin
This creative, delightful narrative is power packed with perspectives from a wide range of happiness promoters. She

also has a terrific blog filled with practical, fun, and meaningful exercises for enjoying life and embracing the moment: http:// gretchenrubin.com/.

✓ *The Last Lecture* by Randy Pausch
This chronicling of Dr. Pausch's personal and professional life is truly moving. Keep the Kleenex handy. You can also view the lecture online. You will love seeing those great big stuffed animals! http://www.cmu.edu/randyslecture/.

✓ *The Short Bus: A Journey Beyond Normal* by Jonathan Mooney
An epic memoir, his story, along with those he features, is gripping and transformative. You'll never think of "normal" in the same way—which is a very good thing. http://www. jonathanmooney.com/

✓ *Spark and Go WILD: Free Your Body and Mind from the Afflictions of Civilization* by John Ratey
If you want ammunition on exercising, Dr. Ratey will fire you up. Both of these books get us thinking about what our bodies are meant to do and the importance of movement for all of the dimensions of health, especially brain function and emotional regulation: http://www.sparkinglife.org/.

✓ *Strengths Finder 2.0* by Tom Rath
As the name implies, this quick read brings us on a scavenger hunt for finding strengths and building upon them. It's got a nifty online self-assessment component tool: http://www. strengthsfinder.com/home.aspx.

✓ *Switch: How to Change Things When Change Is Hard* by Chip Heath and Dan Heath
What did their parents feed them for breakfast? These dynamic brothers bring their readers to new levels of insight as they craft a compelling case for leveraging intellectual and emotional prowess. It's a difficult book to put it down—and

when you finally have to, you'll want to read more of their work, which they've conveniently made available on their website: http://heathbrothers.com/.

✓ *Walking Your Blues Away: How to Heal the Mind and Create Emotional Well-Being* by Thom Hartmann
Known for his crafting of the "hunter/farmer" metaphor in the ADD/ADHD community, Dr. Hartmann offers another delightful framework to help harness human potential. This simple yet scientific read is an absolute gem. In his usual brilliant fashion, Dr. Hartmann crafts a compelling case for walking, offering ideas about how to "walk with problems" in a way that helps us process more effectively. This play-by-play of the neuroscience is fascinating and motivating. Dr. Hartmann has written many other books, ranging from the world of ADD/ADHD to JFK. Check out more at: http://www.thomhartmann.com/thom/books.

✓ *You Mean I'm Not Lazy, Stupid or Crazy?!: The Classic Self-Help Book for Adults with Attention Deficit Disorder* by Kate Kelly and Peggy Ramundo
These two therapists know a thing or two about ADD/ADHD, but not just because of their professional lens. This is a must-read story of two amazing women who know firsthand the perils and beauty of having ADD/ADHD. Their creativity and useful illustrations resonate, whether you have true ADD/ADHD or just need some ideas about juggling life's demands. Sadly, Kate passed away from cancer, but her life's work is a legacy worth celebrating.

INDEX

Page numbers followed by *n* indicate note numbers.

stress and stomach problems and, 168

surgery, 5–6

Health disparities, definition of, 61

"Healthy People 2020," 60

Hedonic treadmill, 110–111

definition of, 110

Hallowell, Edward, 81

Holiday gatherings, 98

Human capital, 145

definition of, 141

Humor, 196

Hyperthyroidism, 7

Hypothyroidism, 6–7

I

If only thought process, 109–110, 112–115, 120–121

Illness, 175–176, 178

Independence, resilience and, 129

Injuries, 175–176, 178

Insecurities, 96

Intake, 90

Intellectual gifts, 69

Interpersonal effectiveness, 86–88

definition of, 87

IQ, 29

J

Judgment, 96, 106

K

Kahneman, Daniel, 152

Kelly, Kate, 81

Kobasa, Suzanne C., 123n46

Kubler-Ross, Elisabeth, 74–75

L

Laughter, 131–133, 196

Library, 192

Life coaches, 65–66

Linehan, Marsha, 79–81

Loneliness, 205–206

Lovecky, Dr. Deirdre V., 70

M

Magical thinking, 108–121, 153

Mantra, 192–196

definition of, 193

examples of, 194

selection of, 195–196

Maslow's hierarchy of needs, 34

Massage, 178, 249

"McDonaldization of society," 53

McEwen, Bruce, PhD, 124n47

Medication

amounts of, 57–59

for anxiety, 26n8

long-term, 57

for mental health issues, 56–59

weight gain with, 57

Meetings, 97

Men, support and, 49–50

Mental filtering, 99–100, 106

case examples of, 100

definition of, 99

Mental health

diagnostic spectrum of, 76–78

education about issues concerning, 50, 56

nonpsychological impacts on, 50–52

Obama and, 142–143

parity in, 145

ABOUT THE AUTHOR

Dr. Kristen Lee Costa, affectionately known as "Dr. Kris," helps people design practical plans to manage stress and adapt to change. With twenty years' experience as a clinical social worker and educator, she is devoted to promoting well-being and leveraging human potential. Dr. Kris is the lead faculty for behavioral sciences, and a Doctor of Education faculty member for Organizational Leadership Studies at Northeastern University in Boston. She operates a clinical and consulting practice devoted to preventing and treating burnout. Dr. Kris lives in Westport, Massachusetts, with her husband and two children.

Also available at www.reset24-7.com:

- User guides for mental health clinicians, educators, and leaders

- User guides for book clubs

CPSIA information can be obtained at www.ICGtesting.com
Printed in the USA
BVOW09s2014061114

374041BV00006B/12/P